DATE DUE | MAR 0 6

GAYLORD			PRINTED IN U.S.A.

"The difficult art of painting comes closer to the divine than any other, since it enables everything to be experienced that God created ..."

Goya in his report to the Academy, 1792

"… painting holds no secrets, but depends only on natural talent, study and *rázon* which, together, produce the greatest achievements in art …"

Goya in a letter to Pedro Cevallos, 7 February 1801

The Picnic, 1776–88
see page 143

"I'm not moaning, nor thinking of moaning, for I believe that no one is richer than he who is content with what he has, and that I am …"

Goya in a letter to Martin Zapater, 20 October 1781

La Novillada, 1780
see page 57

"If anyone wants anything from me, they must come to me; I'm going to be difficult to get hold of and, unless it is for a prominent person or a commission for a friend, I'm not going to work for anyone."

Goya in a letter to Martin Zapater, August 1786

Portrait of the Duchess of Alba, 1797
see page 81

"In order to occupy my imagination which has been painfully preoccupied with my illness and to compensate in part for some of the considerable expenses I have incurred, I have dedicated myself to painting a set of cabinet pictures in which I have been able to include observations of subjects which in general are offered no place in commissioned work and in which there is no room for fantasy and invention …"

Goya in a letter to Bernardo de Yriate, 4 January 1794

The Comedians, 1793
see page 147

"I have made myself so much in demand, they don't stop coming to me ... I don't know how I shall be able to cope, for it's so unexpected that you can hardly imagine it."

Goya in a letter to Martin Zapater, August 1786

The Parasol, 1777
see pages 54/55

"What a profound and impenetrable mystery is locked up in the imitation of divine nature, without which there is nothing good!"

Goya in his report to the Academy, 1792

The Summer, 1786/87
see pages 144/45

"He had no master other than the powers of his imagination and profited the most from observing the techniques used by other artists and from the study of famous works of art in Rome and Spain."

Goya in his chronology for the Prado catalogue, 1826

Infante Francisco de Paula Antonio, 1800

"I had three masters:

Rembrandt, Velázquez and Nature."

Goya in his chronology for the Prado catalogue, 1826

Portrait of the Marquesa de Santa Cruz, 1805
see pages 72/73

"… I have neither good sight nor a steady hand and neither pen nor inkwell, everything fails me except my will …"

Goya in a letter to Joaquín Ferrer, 20 December 1825

Loyalty, drawing for *Los Disparates 17*
1819–23

"Yes, you're right ...

I paint as if I were possessed."

Goya in a letter to Martin Zapater, 19 November 1788

Flying Witches, 1797/98
see page 62

"The author is dreaming. His only intention is to banish harmful superstition and to perpetuate with this work of fancy the sound testimony of Truth."

Written on the preparatory drawing for The Sleep of Reason Produces Monsters, *1797/98*

Preparatory drawing for **The Sleep of Reason Produces Monsters,** *Los Caprichos 43,* 1797/98
see page 147

"I'm not afraid of witches, hobgoblins, apparitions, boastful giants, knaves or varlets, et cetera, nor indeed of any kind of beings except human beings ..."

Goya in a letter to Martin Zapater, undated

For this you were born, *Desastres de la Guerra 12*
see page 110

"There are no rules in painting."

Goya in his report to the Academy, 1792

The Arrest of Christ, 1798
see page 148

"… There is also some merit in the person who … manages to put before the human eye forms and attitudes that have hitherto existed only in the human mind, clouded and confused by lack of understanding or influenced by uncontrollable passions."

From Goya's announcement for Los Caprichos, *1799*

Asmodea, 1820–23
see page 152

"Goya, in gratitude to his friend Arrieta, for the compassion and treatment that saved him from the terrible and dangerous illness which he suffered in late 1819 in his seventy-third year. He painted this in 1820."

Self-Portrait with Dr. Arrieta, 1820
see page 153

I, Goya

By Dagmar Feghelm

PRESTEL

Munich · Berlin · London · New York

Contents

I, Goya

"I shall not need much furniture for my place, for I think that with a print of the Virgin of the Column [Na Sa del Pilar], a table, five chairs, a frying pan, wine-bag, guitar and a spit and lamp, anything else would be superfluous."

In this description of his envisaged home in Zaragoza, to be furnished by his childhood friend Martín Zapater, it is as though Goya is picturing in his mind's eye a Spanish still life, rather like the *bodegones* of Velázquez. At the age of thirty-four, Goya had returned from Madrid to his home town in Aragón. Eight years after his first tentative but generally satisfactory beginnings in decorating the ceiling of the *coreto* (little choir) of the Basílica del Pilar in Zaragoza, he had now been commissioned to decorate the central cupola itself. What satisfaction he must have felt at reaping the fruits of success in the very town where he had grown up in such humble conditions as the fourth of six children born to a gilder whose Midas touch as a craftsman unfortunately did not extend to his private life, dying as he did in poverty.

Goya may have reminisced about his apprenticeship under José Luzan, his difficult beginnings as a painter, his unsuccessful participation as a rank outsider in the competitions of the Royal Academy Madrid, and the journey he had undertaken to Italy in 1771/72, with no financial assistance of any kind, to study the art of that country. On his return from Italy, he married Josefa, sister of the artist Francisco Bayeu – whether out of affection or calculation must remain a moot point. It was undoubtedly an advantageous match, for his curmudgeonly brother-in-law was not only director of Madrid's Real Academia de Bellas Artes but also *pintor de cámara* – painter to the royal court of Carlos III. In fact, it was thanks to him that Goya was commissioned to create the tapestry cartoons that he had been submitting to the Real Fábrica de Tapices de Santa Bárbara over a period of five years, together with his painstakingly listed invoices – which were paid anything but promptly. But this was, at least, a start, and his election to the Real Academia de Bellas Artes de San Fernando in Madrid a few months previously had marked yet another important step on his path – to what? The life-sized *Christ on the Cross* that he had presented with his application for membership of the Real Academia had been a huge challenge to him. He had compromised, or rather disguised, his style: the smoothly executed ideal body with the

Portrait of Zapater (1797)
Over a period of twenty-four years, Goya wrote to his former school friend in Zaragoza. The enlightened, wealthy landowner and businessman faithfully kept the letters. "Dearest Martin" was Goya´s confidant, hunting companion and financial advisor: "… tell me where my 100,000 should best be kept, in the bank or in bonds?"

Self-Portrait in the Studio (1790/95)
Goya's son Javier relates that Goya worked mainly in the mornings and "to achieve the best effect, made the last brushstrokes at night by candlelight." Both are documented here – the morning light and the candles on his hat for evening work.

Portrait of Bayeu (c. 1780)
Though they might not have seen eye to eye about art, Goya's conservative brother-in-law had a strong sense of family loyalty and, by recommending Goya to Anton Raphael Mengs, helped him secure an income designing tapestry cartoons.

Cupola Fresco of El Pilar (1780/81)
"When I think of Zaragoza and of painting, I am consumed with fury ..." Public criticism of his frescoes in the Cathedral of El Pilar deeply wounded Goya's pride.

saccharine Guido Reni gaze may be a superb example of academic classicism, but it does not betray the distinctive hand of the artist. Indeed, it might just as easily be a painting by Anton Raphael Mengs, the grand old man of official Madrid art, who had died recently, or even by Bayeu, under whose roof and disapproving eye Goya had been living in Madrid these past six years. How tempting the call to Zaragoza must have seemed to him at this time. Not that he would not escape Bayeu there entirely, either. After all, he had been asked to complete a project that his busy brother-in-law had been procrastinating over for years. Still, Goya must have looked forward to a little more freedom, both in his art and in his private life – and it had been a long time indeed since he had gone hunting with his friends.

Things did not get off to an auspicious start. The fledgling *académico merito* was deemed to have taken rather too much artistic licence in the eyes of the clerics who ate out of his brother-in-law's hand. Not only did they find the figure of the Virgin enthroned amid martyrs all too gloomy, sketchy and poorly finished, but they also accused him of portraying the figures of saints in the spandrels without the appropriate degree of respect. In short, he had not painted in the 'correct' style. Having struggled for seventeen years to gain recognition as an academic *profesór* and having, finally, gained admission to the illustrious circles of the Academy, this insult proved too much for Goya. He was enraged by the vitriol of public criticism. The longest known document written by Goya is his defence against the accusations levelled at him. He talks of slander and repeatedly of honour, for "a master's reputation is a thing of great delicacy." The injured pride of a man who valued his artistic freedom above all else made it impossible for him to accept orders from his peers, least of all from his 'colleague' Bayeu. Goya even fell out, albeit temporarily, with his longstanding friend Zapater. It was only the religious authority and worldly wisdom of a kindly Carthusian monk that finally persuaded him to relent 'in the spirit of Christian humility'.

Until well after the turn of the century, Goya walked a fine line between career ambition and the desire for artistic freedom. He succeeded admirably. On the one hand, there was the royal court that regarded painters as little more than servants for the production of stiffly formal portraits and ostentatious decoration, hiring and firing them at will. Carlos III managed to get through seven court painters in twenty-nine years, and Carlos IV appointed twenty-six in just nineteen years. On the other hand, there was the lure of an Academy that nurtured classicism and the emulation of the noble ideals of Antiquity. It was a doctrine to which the pragmatic Goya paid his respects for the last time in his *Christ on the Cross* of 1780.

Twelve years later, by which time he was Deputy Director of Painting, he presented an audacious report to the Academy stating the impossibility of learning art by slavishly copying drawings and plaster models. Somewhat surprisingly, this did not hinder his appointment as Director of the Academy in 1795. Meanwhile, he continued to

Christst on the Cross
(1780)
Never did Goya pay such lip service to aesthetic convention as in this work submitted with his application for membership of the Academy. The obvious borrowings from Velázquez, Reni and Mengs make this painstakingly executed neo-classicist painting a masterpiece of pragmatic eclecticism.

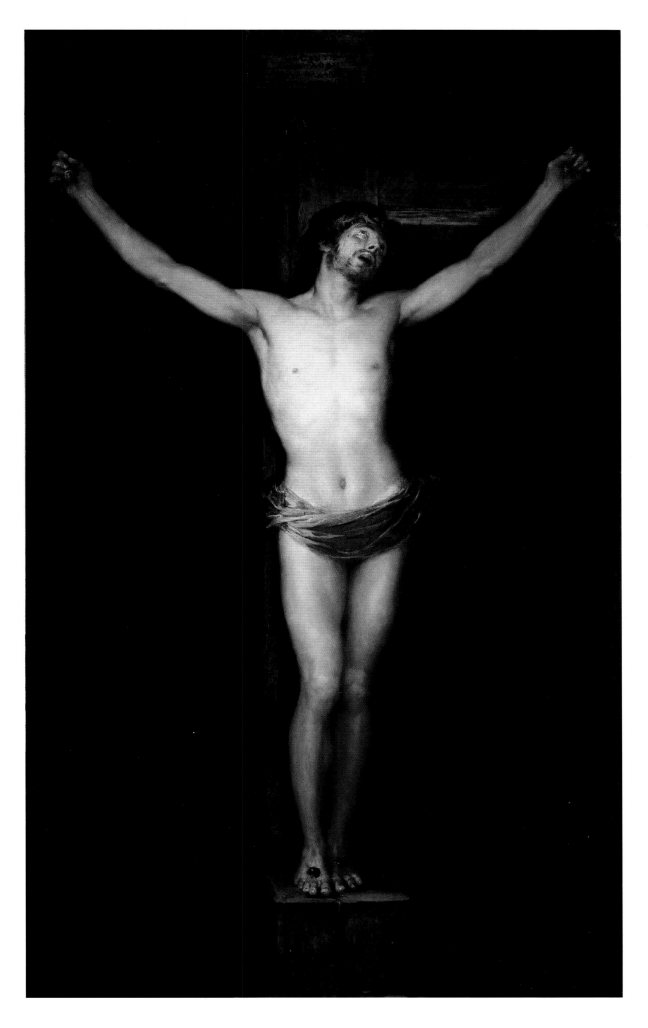

pursue his career at court. In 1786 he became *pintor del rey* – painter to the king – under Carlos III, then in 1789 *pintor de cámara* – court painter – to Carlos IV, and finally, at the age of fifty-three, First Court Painter. He reported these career moves with undisguised satisfaction to his friend: "My dear Martín, I am Painter to the King with 15,000 *reales*…" You can almost hear him blustering with pride and it makes you wonder whether fame or money was more important to him. Whichever it was, he promptly set about purchasing a carriage *à l'anglaise* which he described to his friend right down to the details of its finely gilded decor, including the accident in which he managed to wreck the new gig on his very first outing.

He was not averse to collecting titles either. In 1777 he even started signing his name Francisco di Goya – a title of minor nobility inherited from his mother's side of the family. As soon as he became a member of the Academy, he insisted on being addressed as *profesór* and his appointment as Director of the Academy delighted him every bit as much as the regular income it entailed. In this respect, the human folly he was later to depict in his *Caprichos* was all too familiar to him personally. There is more than a touch of self-irony in his sarcastic portrayals of Vanity, Ambition and Aristocratic Pride. But for the moment, at least, he was still delighted at every favour bestowed upon him by the grandees of his social circle and trumpeted to his friend in Zaragoza that "… the King and the Prince and the Princess, by the Grace of God, gave me the honour of showing them four of my paintings and I kissed their hands. Never before have I had such good fortune." He had never been happier before. He enthused: "The honoured gentlemen are angels," and "Yes, you are right, I am a devil of a painter!" He took a childish delight in being a sought-after artist with commissions pouring in. "My friend, I assure you that I carry these drawings around with me all day long and I rush and do not rest until I have finished." The drawings in question were preliminary studies for a wall tapestry intended for the royal children's nursery. In 1788, Goya's main occupation still consisted in designing cartoons for tapestries and it was to be some time before he would manage to cast off what he increasingly came to regard as a rather degrading duty. "I don't really like providing drawings for others to use," he wrote dejectedly in 1777. He found the work uninspiring and wearying. "Of my own invention," he noted proudly on his invoices from 1776 onwards for designs so original that they were sometimes sent back to him for revision because they were unfeasible. "I wouldn't have to care a fig for what others may think, just do [i.e. paint] what I like…," he wrote in a letter of 1781 with undertones of the sense of dissatisfaction that was only to increase as time went on, adding, "…and let those who involve themselves in intrigues at the court stay in their own muck, for it is clear to me that the covetous neither live nor know where they live." In his reference to life at court, riddled as it was with intrigue, he touched upon another topic that was often on his mind. He developed a growing dislike of the obsequious

Carlos III as Hunter (*c.* 1786–88)
The king from the House of Bourbon supported domestic reforms in the spirit of enlightened Absolutism.

toadying expected of him at the royal court and, by the time he was made court painter in 1789, his joy was mixed with doubts, as indicated in his report that: "A rearing horse will either leap the barrier or tear it down." Finally, around 1790, weary of the hustle and bustle of court life, he wrote these tired, solemn and somewhat cryptic words to Zapater: "I have got it into my mind to uphold a certain idea and retain a certain dignity that one has to have."

Ultimately, it was Goya's friends who were to uphold the idea and the dignity – foremost among them a number of enlightened intellectuals, some in high positions, who sought to disseminate the ideas of Rousseau, Voltaire and Diderot. That was no easy task in a land so hopelessly backward, where absolute power was in the hands of crown and church, and where the predominantly rural population lived in abject poverty, ignorance, superstition and fear of the Inquisition.

At the *tertulias*, as the casual gatherings of these intellectual *ilustrados* were known, Goya may well have found support and confirmation – both in philosophy and literature – for the views and opinions he himself had formed on the basis of his own common sense and awareness of human nature. Here, he found himself in the company of others who also agreed that it was not enough merely to ban masked bandits from bearing weapons or wearing capes and wide-brimmed hats, nor enough simply to found a state bank or drive out the Jesuits, as the reformist Carlos III had sought to do in 1766/67. Carlos' own pet project, the beautification of Madrid with new promenades, grottoes and fountains, may have provided a graceful backdrop for the *majos* and *majas* and picturesque motifs for the wall tapestries that graced the royal chambers – but it could hardly have been said to tackle the core problems. All this was little more than short-sighted *reformismo borbónico*. Under Carlos IV, even these modest reforms ground to a halt, and they did so from 1789 onwards, just as events in France were firing the imagination of Spanish liberals. One of those Spanish liberals was Goya himself. He painted all their portraits, finding a firm foothold in this circle of friends and patrons who not only possessed a thorough knowledge of art, but also had the means with which to purchase it. Soon, his academic colleagues were becoming envious of the high prices that Goya commanded – and received – for his portraiture.

Had Goya died in 1792/93 when he was suddenly struck down by a serious illness in Andalusia, posterity might have mourned an artist who had frittered away his talents in the service of an Ancien Régime court, producing decorative designs that were no more and no less than a somewhat idiosyncratic swansong to Rococo.

He did indeed have a close brush with death in those months. Exactly what it was that ailed him, tormenting him with agonising colic, headaches and dizziness, remains shrouded in mystery – though it was to be embellished by later legends, some of them based among other things on Zapater's letter to Bayeu mentioning "Goya's

El paseo de Andalucia (1777)
The *paseo de Andalucia* is the Spanish variation on the French *fête galante*. With its swaggering majos, this scene verges on a cloak-and-dagger operetta.

The San Isidro Meadows (1788)
In this small oil sketch, Goya presents a broad panorama of Madrid. The city itself, its skyline rendered in minute detail, seems as festive as the locals enjoying a picnic in celebration of the 15 May feast day of San Isidro, patron saint of Madrid. The parasol in the foreground skilfully draws the viewer's eye towards the new royal palace on the opposite bank of the Manzanares.

carelessness … that has brought things to this pass." It had certainly been careless of him to undertake the journey without court leave, and it had taken a considerable amount of effort on the part of Bayeu and Sebastian Martínez, the friend in Cadiz who took the invalid in for six months, to cover up for this indiscretion. The news that Goya had been left deaf by his illness may have helped his case at court, and on his return he informed the tapestry manufactory that he was 'quite incapable of painting' – though this applied only to the tapestry cartoons he so detested. The crisis had left him drained of energy, both physically and mentally. "Sleep," he wrote to Zapater, is "a remedy I resort to when depression overwhelms me." His convalescence was also aided by painting scenes of bullfights and the theatre, natural catastrophes and the yard of an insane asylum which he sent to the Academy in 1794. "In order to occupy my imagination which has been painfully preoccupied with my illness and to compensate in part for some of the considerable expenses I have incurred, I have dedicated myself to painting a set of cabinet pictures in which I have been able to include observations of subjects which in general are offered no place in commissioned work and in which there is no room for fantasy and invention."

As so often in Goya's life, pragmatism and creative genius went hand in hand here. For the first time, he was painting whatever he wanted. It was almost as though his deafness allowed him at last to ignore what the world demanded of him. He did not – could not – listen. Yet he never lost sight of his accounts. Fear of poverty drove him all his life. It seems odd that he should have seen fit to present the fruits of this act of liberation to none other than the very institution from which he could surely have expected the least favourable response. When the works were received with unexpected acclaim, he wrote back declaring: "I have renewed my intention to apply myself with enthusiasm to produce works worthy of so honourable an institution," as though relieved to find his transgressions forgiven and his artistic caprices condoned. Could the crisis have been a blessing in disguise after all? Perhaps the journey – ostensibly occasioned by a church commission in Cadiz – had been an attempt to break free, as had the provocative report he had sent, shortly before his departure, to the Academy and its high priests who worshipped plaster-cast gods.

At any rate, having narrowly escaped death, he now seemed eager to avoid all unwelcome obligations and to pursue the essential things in art and life. In this, he grasped a rare opportunity to make an unusual observation by looking over his own shoulder, so to speak, as he fell head over heels in love.

His affair with the Duchess of Alba ended in tears. As befits a *cortejo*, he maintained his dignity in the face of his beloved's infidelity. But the *Caprichos* he created around this time contain any number of coded references to the deceitfulness and fickleness of women. The series published in 1799 is also the personal inventory of a specific phase in his life. Indeed, Goya seems to have had something of a passion for

Yard of the Madhouse (1794)
This scene is one of the uncommissioned cabinet pieces that Goya painted after he went deaf. In the yard, enclosed by high walls like a prison, a fight has broken out. But the manic eyes of most of the inmates are focused on the viewer, who takes the position of an onlooker. In Goya's day, visiting an insane asylum was a popular, if macabre, pastime.

Portrait (drawing) of Josefa Bayeu (1805)
The only known portrait of Goya's wife
shows her at the age of fifty-eight.
Goya appreciated Josefa's wit and the
humour with which she faced adversity.
For instance, she described the house
in Zaragoza that Zapater had procured
for the family in 1780 as 'a sepulchre
for women' because of its location in a
gloomy part of town.

Portrait of Mariano Goya (c. 1815)
Goya painted his eight-year-old grandson
Mariano in sober black with a white lace
collar, lending the boy's finely featured
face all the more freshness and vitality
against the grey background.

inventorising at this time, putting his life in order and rearranging it. In 1800 he sold
one house and bought two others. Then, in 1803, he presented the unsold copies of
the *Caprichos*, together with the printing plates, to the king in return for a pension for
his son. The pension was granted, but Javier never undertook the envisaged study
tour. Goya's sole surviving child was reticent and spoilt and could think of nothing
better to do with his life than become a painter who did not paint. In 1805, the
twenty-year-old Javier married a merchant's daughter by the name of Gumersinda
and settled down to a life of leisure at the cost of his indulgent, adoring and perhaps
somewhat disappointed father. For their wedding, Goya, apparently blinded by pater-
nal pride, painted full-figure swagger portraits of the elegant couple. There followed
by a series of sketchy, life-like portrait miniatures of the immature and sullen-looking
pair, of all the bride's family, and a sombre drawing of the matronly Josefa in aloof
profile. This seemed to conclude the visual inventory of the extended family.

By the age of sixty, Goya had achieved all he could have hoped to achieve. He was
unrivalled at court and a celebrated society portraitist. Like Velázquez before him,
whom he profoundly admired, he had painted the official portrait of the royal family
whose approval he had won. He had ensured the wellbeing of his siblings in Zaragoza
and his family in Madrid. He could now retire, enjoying his favourite drink of choco-
late with his grandson Mariano and devoting his energies entirely to his artistic
'moods and inventions', his dreams and visions and his portrayals of all the 'forms
and poses' that he mentions in his announcement of the *Caprichos* as having "existed
previously in the darkness and confusion of an irrational mind, or one which is beset
by uncontrolled passion."

But by now the confusion of the irrational mind was taking on a collective form. By
the latest in 1808, when Napoleon's army marched in, world politics had broken
through the protective *cordon sanitaire* of the Pyrenees. The wheel of fate was turning
at terrifying speed. Manuel Godoy, triumphant protégé of the royal court at the zenith
of his political career, was dragged down along with the king and queen. And it was
not the royal heir Ferdinand who succeeded to the throne, but Joseph Bonaparte,
brother of the 'parvenue from that godless neighbouring country'. The consequences
were dire. What began in May 1808 as an uprising against the invading army and went
down in history as the Spanish War of Independence may be regarded as the first
modern war – five long years of brutal guerilla warfare by the people against the occu-
pying forces. More than ever before, it was the tide of time that shaped Goya's life and
art. He could not take an unequivocal stance. As a liberal, he may have been happy to
see Joseph Bonaparte sweep aside the Inquisition along with feudal privileges and
church wealth, but as a Spaniard he was patriotic enough to want to see the back of
the French invaders and, as an individual, he was humane enough to be shocked at the
harrowing cruelty of war.

Portrait of Wellington (1812/14)
Wellington had neither the time nor the inclination to sit for a portrait. Goya completed the painting in just three weeks, based on a red chalk study – but he had to constantly update the many medals adorning Wellington's uniform.

Equestrian Portrait of Palafox (1814)
In a letter of 1794 Goya described this as "...one of the most difficult subjects any painter may be confronted with." Although he had by now painted many portraits, only a war hero such as General Palafox shared with their royal majesties the honour of having a full-size portrait done.

Once again, he found himself treading the thinnest of lines: he wanted to retain his status as court painter, but he also wanted to make a stand against hatred, brutality and inhumanity. And so he painted for all those who briefly stood upon the stage of power in Spain: he painted for King Joseph and the Spanish General Palafox, for that scourge of the French, Wellington, and for the Infante Ferdinand who was so adulated by the people but whose coronation in 1814 heralded the advent of a regime more reactionary than anything Spain had ever seen before. Goya himself had to answer to the re-instated Inquisition for his *Naked Maja* and *Clothed Maja*, which were found among the confiscated possessions of the 'Prince of the Peace' Manuel Godoy. Once again, Goya escaped.

Though unscathed by the witchhunt unleashed against liberals, it left its mark on him psychologically. Fundamentally, his exile in 1824 had its beginnings in those years. Even when he began his *Desastres de la Guerra* cycle of etchings depicting the horrors of war in 1810, he clearly did not have publication in mind. The inventory of seventy-eight pictures in his house, drawn up by his wife Josefa for their son on Goya's death in 1812, indicates that he had long since become his own best patron, at least as far as portrayals of sexuality, cruelty and violence were concerned. All ten of Goya's still-lifes were in his own private collection and their morbid gloominess dovetails perfectly with his very personal choice of motifs. The first step from inner exile to actual emigration was taken in 1819 with the purchase of a country house on the outskirts of Madrid. Just as he had become seriously ill on his first attempt to flee an unbearable life, so too did he now succumb to illness, and his self-portrait with his doctor indicates that he showed very little resistance to it. The ghosts that had haunted him in his struggle with death never left him. He captured them in nightmarish depictions on the walls of the house that had already come to be known locally – due to a previous owner – as the *Quinta del Sordo*, or 'house of the deaf man'. Only a young woman, immersed in thought, brings a speck of light into these Black Paintings. She is Leocadia, a relative from the family of his daughter-in-law. Although married, Leocadia had lived there with Goya for some time. He depicts her leaning against what looks like the mound of a grave, possibly as an expression of his yearning for death; but he still had several eventful years ahead of him.

Spain showed no signs of calming. Whereas, in 1820, the ageing Enlightenment thinkers, most of them now living in exile and known disparagingly as *afrancescados*, had still nurtured hopes that they might yet see the implementation of the reforms outlined in the 1812 Constitution of Cadiz, these hopes were dashed again when an army of the ultra-reactionary Holy Alliance marched into Spain at the request of Ferdinand. The victory of these hundred thousand sons of Louis the Sacred in 1823 unleashed a period of repression and restriction that did not abate until Ferdinand's death in 1833 which finally sealed the fate of the liberals. With his own openly liberal

Plucked Turkey (*c.* 1808/12)
In a bold diagonal, the up-ended turkey
dominates this gloomy scene. Its naked,
twisted body and the wan shimmer of its
dead flesh epitomise the notion of violent
death. Though Goya's still life studies are
consistent with Spanish artistic tradition,
he imbued them with an expressiveness
that remained unparalleled until the
modern era.

views, the no less liberal Leocadia at his side and such unseemly works as the *Desastres* in his home, Goya, at the age of seventy-seven, found himself in a very precarious position indeed.

Yet another inventory and a new beginning were on the cards and, once again, Goya was tormented by his liberal leanings and his persistence in clinging to his status as court painter. In 1823 he bequeathed his country house to his grandson, but instead of leaving the country, he went into hiding at the home of a friend, only to petition the court a few months later to be allowed to take a cure at Plombières in France for the good of his ailing health – a request that was immediately granted. Ferdinand may have been a despot, but to Goya he proved a magnanimous patron who unquestioningly continued his payments while he was in exile. Goya travelled first to Paris, then in late 1824 to Bordeaux, which had long given refuge to Spanish liberals. "Goya plagues me and doesn't give me a moment's peace," writes his old friend Moratín. "He is here with his Dona Leocadia. I cannot discern the slightest harmony between them." It would seem that Goya, by now the gruff old man of his 1824 self-portrait, had found in Leocadia a character as strong-willed and stubborn as himself. As Moratín writes, "Since he has been here, he has not been troubled by any illness. Nevertheless, he sometimes gets it into his head that he has a lot to do in Madrid and, were he allowed to have his own way, he would set off with a stubborn donkey, his peasant's hat, his cape, his wooden stirrups, his wine-skin and his knapsack." And indeed, he did set off on the ten-day journey two more times – once in 1826 to request retirement on full pay which was granted. Moratín's grimly affectionate comment on this was: "He travels alone, full of rancour at the French. If he does not arrive, this will come as no surprise, for at the slightest illness he might end up dead in some corner of an inn."

Yet Goya still had huge reserves of energy, as his paintings from these years demonstrate. For one last time, he paraded the key themes of his art. By now, he was finding it difficult to paint, for, as he said: "I am lacking in everything, in eyesight, strength, pens, ink – all that remains is willpower." He wrote this in a letter to a friend in 1825, enclosing a set of four prints known collectively as the *Bulls of Bordeaux*, involving the relatively new technique of lithography technique that he already felt too old to experiment with. His 1824/28 *Aun aprendo* (I am still learning) shows a beady-eyed old man walking on crutches; it is mulishly obstinate and self-assured, full of curiosity and lust for life – 'still learning' means still living. Living and learning were one and the same to Goya.

La Leocadia (1820/23)
In 1873 Goya's Black Paintings were removed from the walls of the Quinta del Sordo and transferred to canvas. In the process, the face, or rather the gaze, of Leocadia was heavily restored. In the air of mourning that hangs over the woman who was Goya's companion during the final years of his life, youth and death seem to meld into a metaphor of melancholy.

Aun aprendo…
I am still learning, 1825–1828
Shortly before his death Goya portrayed himself as an aging monk on a pilgrimage.

Colourful Life

"What a scandal to hear nature deprecated in comparison to Greek statues by one who knows neither one nor the other without acknowledging that the smallest part of Nature confounds and amazes those who know most! What statue or cast of it might there be that is not copied from divine nature?"

From Goya's report to the Academy, 1792

Goya was always interested in street life. Even in the last years of his life, he continued to document some of the odd means of transport he had seen on his travels. Alongside the painstaking drapery studies in his Italian sketchbook we find a woman gracefully carrying a basket, drawn with strong and rapid strokes as though the artist were taking a breath of fresh air after the stultifying chore of drawing fold upon fold in the studio. Yet before our very eyes the woman with the basket seems to turn into a statuesque Vestal Virgin in oils who appears to be shivering in spite of the fire – just as the artist himself appears to have been unable to warm to the demands of the classical canon of forms.

Back in Zaragoza, Goya demonstrated in his commissions for the church what he had learned on his travels: a painterly style full of light and motion in the manner of the Neapolitan Late Baroque of Giordano and Giaquinto for all things celestial, and a more ponderously modelled monumental style in the manner of Poussin and Vouet for depictions of earthly redemption.

Equipped with these skills, he arrived in Madrid under the tutelage of Bayeu. At the time, Carlos III was undertaking a programme of decoration for the new palace and other royal residences, for which he had commissioned two celebrated artists, Tiepolo and Mengs, but their respective approach to painting could hardly have differed more. This remained, in fact, unaltered right up until Tiepolo's death in 1770. The two artists worked independently on their frescoes and altarpieces with polite mutual disdain. The more profane tasks were left to local artists and the most profane of all – designing tapestry cartoons – was left to Goya. Carlos III loved to hunt – as did Goya, and this worked to his advantage in the first of his cartoons, which were hunting scenes created under the guidance of his brother-in-law. Carlos IV and Queen María Luisa, who were to make Goya their court painter in 1789, preferred to decorate their chambers with lively folk scenes, and Goya indulged in a little joke of his own by depicting himself as a *torero*.

From the Bordeaux Albums (1824–28)
The Bordeaux Albums include a group of drawings showing bizarre forms of transport that were actually used at the time.

Page 52
Dancers on the Banks of the Manzanares (1777)
What looks like a bucolic minuet is in fact the *seguidilla* – a Spanish folk dance whose stately rhythm is echoed here in the lovely landscape. In the background is the skyline of Madrid, which had a population of about 145,000 in the mid-eighteenth century.

"Look what I can do!" his gaze seems to be saying as he brandishes the *capa* with all the flamboyance of his brushstroke, which had become so much freer since Bayeu stopped looking over his shoulder constantly. The sketch-like figures behind the walls are particularly fine – but what on earth is a tapestry weaver supposed to do with these? The square areas of wall, the narrow corner strips, the lintels viewed from below – complex as the format itself may be, the compositional requirements of designing light-hearted and decoratively pleasing tapestries placed considerable restraints on an artist of Goya's temperament. But at least they did not demand a classicistic approach. The flirtatious beauty in a silk dress is certainly more suited to Goya than the classically cool Vestal Virgin, and the coquettish parasol gives him ample opportunity to play with the effects of light – but what is the point of the exercise if all this subtlety is to be lost in the translation to tapestry and the cartoons themselves are to end up languishing in the archives? Nevertheless, the work did have a certain appeal in that it allowed Goya to depict the things he saw with his own eyes – the seductive *majas* with their greedy old *celestinas* in tow, the aloof and enigmatic ladies in their carriages, the arrogant *caballeros*, the servants in their garish livery and the pedlars sitting by the wayside.

Goya took the royal request for colourful scenes that would brighten up the gloomy palace at face value. He trawled the bucolic lyricism of Rococo, portraying such familiar amusements as picnics, dancing and childish games; washerwomen and sheaf-binders dallying and slumbering in eternal youth – Goya had been quick to learn the French idiom. But his mastery of the Spanish idiom was better still. This can be seen first and foremost in his portrayal of Spanish dress, which he mixes with the fashionable French finery of the foppish dandies who were ridiculed as *petimetres*. The young women from Madrid's poorer quarters dressed as though every day were a high holiday. The provocatively dissolute life of *majismo* he presents is both romantic folklore and at the same time a sign of increasing national identity and pride. The new fashion for dressing Andalusian style was adopted by the nobility, even by the queen herself.

When Goya came to Madrid from the provincial town of Zaragoza at the age of twenty-eight, he was still young enough to be fascinated by the picturesque flamboyance of the *majas* and their suitors. His colourfully bawdy folk scenes showing *majos* courting, brawling, smoking and playing guitar soon shifted away from the artificial smoothness of the French repertoire. The shimmering sylvan backgrounds made way for realistically barren plateaus and rugged mountain ranges. Cracks began to appear in the *galant monde*. The smile of the revellers in *Dancing on the Banks of the Manzanares* is frozen to a mask in his *Blind Man's Buff* of 1788 as though the players themselves found their pursuits all too childish.

La Novillada (1780)
The bold demeanour of this figure,
presumably a self-portrait, makes it easy
to understand why there were so many
wild rumours about the young Goya
during his own lifetime. He himself continued to fuel the gossip even in his old age,
by remarking that he had "...fought as a
torero, dagger in hand, fearing nothing."

Pages 54/55
The Parasol (El quitasol) (1777)
The clothing, the fan and the little lapdog
define this woman as a *petimetre* – a
derogatory term for the ruling classes
in reference to their emulation of French
fashions and manners, until even they
succumbed to the charms of the Spanish
majismo.

Page 56
Hunter with Hounds (1775)
The tapestry weaver must surely have
been glad to receive a design so easy to
transpose to wool and silk.

Blind Man's Buff *(1788/89)*
On closer inspection, what appears at first to be a childish game takes on a deeper and more symbolic meaning: the circling movement and the river are symbols of unforeseen fate and passing time. Blind Man's Buff as a symbol of blind fate that chooses and torments its victims at will.

Winter (1786/87)
Goya did not paint this winter scene as a
conventional allegory of the seasons, but
as a grippingly realistic portrayal of the
forces of nature. It is not only the wild
weather, but also people themselves that
pose a threat – the gun recalls the rampant
banditry that turned every journey into a
hazardous undertaking.

The Marriage (1791/92)
Goya has portrayed the age-old theme of
the ill-matched couple in a mordant genre
style redolent of a Hogarth satire. The
wedding procession passes like a frieze
over the arch of a bridge which fames the
unhappy couple, dressed in all their finery,
and the amused onlookers.

The days of children playing at soldiers and grown-ups playing at blind man's buff is over – in France as well as Spain. Even Fragonard, unrivalled in his field, suffered the ignominy of Madame Dubarry rejecting a suite of paintings executed in the loveliest Rococo style. The time had come for the pathos-laden morality of Jacques-Louis David.

In his last cartoons, Goya too turned his back on preening, boastful *majismo* in search of more realistic themes. These he sometimes takes to extremes – as in the tongue-in-cheek sarcasm with which he depicts the marriage of an ill-matched couple. When his tapestry cartoon of a drunken mason was rejected, he reworked it with a few brush strokes into a heart-rending image of an *Injured Mason* being carried by his compassionate workmates. This new wind blows still keener in his portrayal of *Winter* (*The Snowstorm*) in a cycle of the four seasons: poorly clad peasants struggling through the storm to bring home a slaughtered pig on the back of a mule trudge through a polar landscape in a wan twilight. You can almost hear the wind howling and the crunch of footsteps in the snow and find yourself hoping that the wanderers will soon reach their destination. With this scene for the dining hall of the El Pardo palace Goya had completely defied tradition. Not only did such cold, monochromatic colours and harsh, frameless compositions signal the death of tapestry in the conventional sense, but the naturalism and crass reality of the scene went far beyond anything that might be set before even the most populistically inclined of kings – especially when he was dining. Goya broke the rules of decorum. He was no decorative craftsman.

Flying Witches (1797/98)
This, along with the *Witches' Sabbath*, is one of six
cabinet pieces purchased by the Duchess of Osuna
for her country house at Alameda. The tongue-in-
cheek tone in some of these scenes reflects the
enlightened intellectuals' rejection of popular
superstition and, at the same time, their fascination
with it.

Witches' Sabbath (1797/98)
This gruesome scene of a child being sacrificed is based on a literary source which, in turn, comes from an *autodafé* of 1610. The devil is shown in the guise of a goat, which was considered an impure and lascivious beast. Similarly, his satyr-like appearance and the inclusion of vine leaves is a reference to ancient Dionysian rites.

Portrait of Floridablanca (1783)
Prime Minister under Carlos III and Carlos
IV, Floridablanca applied enlightened ideas
to further the Spanish economy. Toppled
by Queen Maria Luisa and Godoy, he died
in exile in 1808. Goya's portrait of him
can also be read as an allegory of good
government.

What he created here was, in a way, a kind of second 'admission piece' – this time marking his joining the ranks of the great realists. Ten years later, the same stubborn mule and one of the wanderers crops up again – this time as a figure covering his head in horror as he flees from an apparation of witches who are carrying off their naked victim into the black night sky (*Flying Witches*, 1797/98). Perhaps Goya was rendering this vision all too realistically in order to excite a real sense of horror – the nocturnal *Witches' Sabbath* in the same series looks more like a perverted counterpoint to *Daydreams of a Trip to the Country* of 1788.

The ground was paved for the imaging of a different, darker world. Goya was to address this world in a way no artist before him had ever done. He would lend a visible reality to the abyss of humankind's inner imagery without ever losing his interest in the outward appearance of the individual.

No matter what bold means he found of portraying the monsters of the subconscious, as a portraitist Goya always remained a firm-footed realist. He quickly grasped portraiture as a reliable way of accruing money and fame. He ambitiously pulled out all the stops to portray the Count of Floridablanca, the first to commission a portrait from him, with all the qualities of a grandee in full-blown Baroque style. In spite of his somewhat archaic and clumsy pose, the minister exudes an air of radiant vitality, with the visionary gaze and optimistic smile of the Enlightenment thinker, standing before a desk littered with papers and scattered books. His plans for a canal project are casually propped on the bureau and a secretary stands ready to put the Count's ideas to paper. He works long hours and serves two masters: the Common Weal and the King, who is enthroned over the scene in an oval painting. The most humble servant of all is Goya himself, rendered far too small, permitted to present a painting. However humbly he may stand there in the shadows, his profile against the strangely lit drapery betrays a remarkable audacity. "We shall talk further," as Goya reported to a friend with some trepidation, had been the Count's only comment on this picture. He knew full well that he had created no masterpiece with this portrait of a gouty, stiff grandsegnieur. The uncertain handling of anatomy, proportion and perspective in this work indicate how even a natural talent such as Goya's could benefit from lessons in academic draughtsmanship.

In the summer months of 1783 and 1784 Goya was invited to Arenas de San Pedro, where the brother of Carlos III was living in rural exile. Don Luis' unsuitable marriage to a commoner, María Teresa de Vallabriga, had pushed him into a lifestyle diametrically opposed to the pomp and ceremony of the Madrid court and, in keeping with his romantic love-match, he presented his home as a Rousseauesque haven of nature. The casually cultivated lifestyle here came as something of a revelation to Goya, who was still unaccustomed to moving in such

social circles. He went hunting with the gentlemen and purportedly received generous gifts – for portraits culminating in an intimate group portrait. The family and servants have gathered together informally around the radiant lady of the house, who is having her magnificent hair styled by a coiffeur while her kindly and elderly husband – according to Casanova a remarkably ugly man – sits contentedly at the table. While the son echoes his father, the little girl precociously scrutinising the artist has the same candid gaze as her mother. The domestic staff are gathered around this core group. Refreshingly naive as this candlelit scene with its earthy colours and lively faces may be, it contains a wealth of references that would have been understood by educated people of that time. Where, indeed, might such an authority as the Swiss scholar Johann Kaspar Lavater have found a more receptive audiencce for his studies on the relationship between physical appearance and character than in such a cultivated circle as this? His *Fragments on*

Family Portrait of Infante Don Luis (1783)
Goya was evidently familiar with reproductions of the English 'conversation pieces' by such artists as Hogarth and Wright of Derby. A remark to Zapater indicates how proud he was of this modern-style picture, which other artists sought in vain to emulate.

Portrait of the Osuna Family (c. 1789)
This progressive and open-minded couple welcomed guests into their home, where they held concerts and plays. In this portrait, the absence of status symbols and the fact that the children are seen as free individuals is indicative of the enlightened lifestyle of the ducal family.

Portrait of Manuel Osorio (c. 1788)
Innocent angel or cheeky little brat? Goya's portraits of children combine the grace of French rococo with a keen eye for psychological subtleties.

Physiognomy for the Promotion of Knowledge and the Love of Mankind may well have been the subject of heated debate and Goya was certainly the man to test on canvas these theories that were a cross between scientific study and parlour game. In this respect, the artificially darkened room can also be seen as the setting for an experiment in which the striking profile of the head of the household indicates blue-blooded royalty while his capricious wife shows the kind of beauty that Lavater's English counterpart Alexander Cozen described as 'majestic'. But Goya's silhouette – which, even in the portrait of the Count had been clearly and deliberately staged – corresponds precisely to Lavater's drawing of a wise man.

This *tour de force* was not in vain. His reputation as a portraitist is evident in a series of portraits of the founder of the San Carlos Bank and the family of the Duke of Osuna, who was one of Goya's most open-minded patrons. After the almost intimate informality of the princely family, the stiff formality of this particular representation seems surprising. It is almost as though Goya were somehow inhibited; his attempt to lend the Duke an air of spontaneity and dynamism makes him look oddly lopsided, and the emaciated arm of the Duchess looks as though it were hanging on a puppetry thread. Yet the portrait has a certain magical charm as if Goya, in executing this painting, had lost his initial reticence and simply dashed off the hair, fabric and lace. It is a finely nuanced rhapsody in grey, like a pastel study in which the splashes of colour light up with the same radiance as the sensitive, porcelain-hued faces. The youngest boy, who was later to become Director of the Prado, sits quietly on his cushion, as well behaved as the three-year-old Manuel Osorio in his portrait of 1788. While the one is pulling a little cart, the other has a magpie on a lead, with three menacingly still cats watching it from the darkened periphery of the room. The child's distinct lack of involvement, his innocent yet patiently expectant gaze – these are as perplexing as the aureola of light behind his head. Might this portrait harbour a visual riddle in reference to the child's name, Emanuel: the redeemer from death and renewer of life? If so, it blends the high ideals of the patron with Goya's keen eye for human nature. There is clearly a negative undertone beneath the child's innocent expression.

The Family of Carlos IV (1800/01)
The reference to Velázquez famous
Las Meninas at the court of Felipe IV
was welcomed by Goya's royal sitters.

It is an ambivalent, even multivalent, enigma in which demonic animals strike the very chord that will later swell to a melody in the *Caprichos*.

Goya painted a third family portrait some ten years later during the turbulent period that was to shape his own life and change the course of history. With the institution of monarchy called into question by the French Revolution, the royal pair may well have made a conscious decision to start the new century by proudly and defiantly documenting the power and continuity of the Spanish Bourbons in a representative painting of the family. This is certainly the central message of the picture painted by Goya shortly after his appointment as First Court Painter, having already immortalised Carlos and María Luisa in all manner of roles – hunting and on horseback, the unattractive and vain, clever and energetic queen in the role of maja and *à la francaise* in a hooped skirt. Some twenty years after the Zaragoza frescoes, Goya was called to the royal summer residence of Aranjuez. It took him an entire year to complete the individual studies for his grand and hierarchically structured tableau of a sober alignment of figures without fussily fluttering draperies – a shockingly modern work.

This time, it was well received by their royal highnesses. The art critic Théophile Gautier, however, saw in the painting nothing but "the local baker and his wife, proud of winning the lottery." There is no shortage of sumptuous –ostentation in the painting, which is teeming with medals and sashes, with glittering diamonds and shimmering fabrics, all painted with a brushstroke so free that the entire room seems to glow with a diffuse light. It would take quite a lot of personal radiance to compete with this – as the vacant expressions of the royal group patently fail to do. Just as, two years previously, Goya had not painted 'proper' angels in his frescoes at San Antonio de la Florida, but simply dubious beauties in the guise of angels, here too, he does not paint a 'proper' dynasty, but merely dressed-up ordinary citizens with all too human traits. The old institutions of crown and church had lost their aura. Goya instinctively captures this. In his painting – where he himself can once again be found peering out of the darkness – what he presents are not caricatures but "this is what I see and I cannot do otherwise." Yet his high-born sitters feel beyond reproach in their ugliness and see only what they want to see: a strong ruling dynasty firmly anchored in the present and future.

Portrait of Manuel Godoy (1801)
The Principe de la Paz was one of Goya's most important patrons, though the artist regarded this powerful man with as much ambivalence as his contemporaries, and indeed posterity. In a letter to Zapater, he enthuses that "he allowed me to keep my coat on during the meal because it was so cold." On another occasion, he mocks Godoy's pompousness. The portrait shows Godoy as the victor in the 'Orange War' against Portugal.

Portrait of Pedro Romero (*c.* 1795/98)
Famous toreros were feted as national
heroes in Spain. One of the greatest of
them all was Pedro Romero. Goya, who
kept a copy of the portrait himself, took
care to emphasise Romero's distinguishing
traits – his grey hair and his steady hand.

Portrait of Isabel de Porcel (1804/05)
The elegant mantilla worn by the wife of the
Castilian Consul indicates the prevalence
of the maja dress even in the highest social
circles. The 1799 law banning brightly
coloured luxury clothing was easily circum-
vented – black lace being an expensive and
coveted import.

Portrait of Contessa Chinchón (1800)
"You can't even see her face for that forest of hair, and I don't want to spoil her mood by telling her I don't like it." Godoy's words to the queen about his wife speak volumes about their marriage. At the age of eighteen, the unfortunate Contessa had been forced into an arranged marriage with the Queen's lover at the latter's insistence.

Pages 72/73
Portrait of Marquesa de Santa Cruz (1805)
It was probably the Marquesa herself who suggested that her portrait be painted in the relaxed pose of Jacques-Louis David's *Madame Recamier*, which was, at the time, *le dernier cri*. The subtle handling of colour makes this painting a masterpiece of its kind.

Goya's success as a portraitist became an obligation. Manuel Godoy – the queen's lover and, to all intents and purposes, regent – even learned sign language in order to communicate with the deaf artist, and was subsequently well pleased with his portrait as an ostensibly victorious military campaigner. Just as Tischbein had portrayed Goethe in the Campagna, here the warrior Prince of the Peace is shown meditating calmly at the edge of the battlefield submerged in romantic gloom behind him. While the sonority of the blue, red and yellow may suggest pomp and circumstance, what we have here is again a case of someone seeing what they want to see; Godoy apparently read the stoutness and smugness of his portrait as strength and masculinity, the blasé indifference as regal stoicism.

On the theme of hero, Goya created counter-models to Godoy in his portrait of the dashing, foolhardily charging Palafox and of the Duke of Wellington, who thought his picture a poor likeness. The portrait of the bullfighter Pedro Romero shows that Goya employed more subtle means of presenting his own personal heroes. Here, skill and daring are not shown in wild action, impeccable uniform or a barrage of medals, but in physical suppleness and a fine hand. The female counterpart to this epitome of a *torero* might be the portrait of Isabel de Porcel – *the* picture of a *maja*, full of sensuality, vitality, beauty and grandezza. Grandezza is a particular characteristic of the women that Goya painted around 1800/1805 with a bold brush and a casual touch – a nonchalance that is transferred to the sitters themselves. Though Goya may have become increasingly misanthropic as he grew older, he clearly never lost the confident attitude of the *majismo*. He rarely departed from the formula of a half-figure portrait on a neutral ground, only using the full-figure portrait to heighten the sense of rank, dignity and aloofness.

For all her simplicity and quietly noble elegance, the shy young Contessa Chinchón portrayed slightly from below has something of an innocently repentant Magdalene. The gaze that sweeps away into the surrounding darkness and the hands clasped in front of the pregnant belly suggest a certain vulnerability, reticence and inner tension, while retaining a studiously self-assured air of dignity.

The Marquesa de Santa Cruz, née Osuna, seems to have retained more of the childhood portrayal. As in the family portrait, she looks at the viewer with a gaze that is disturbingly challenging, and once again she has brought along her favourite plaything. Only now, instead of a spinning top, it is a lyre, its sweeping curves echoing the elegant contour of her pose.

These portraits show Goya's supreme handling of colour and brushwork. Opaque atlas white against mother-of-pearl skin on a cool ground and transparent voile that makes the reddish hue of the flesh, underlined by the upholstery, shimmer warmly – all are subtly distinguished to convey the innocence and dignity (or as Godoy disdainfully put it, the "pathetic and indifferent soul") of the Contessa and the sophisticated eroticism of the Marquesa that translates the vulgarity of the *Clothed Maja* into the language of the aristocracy.

Goya had closely studied the subtle changes of register in the aesthetic vocabulary of such artists as Velázquez, whose grouchy *Aesop* is actually a portrait of his friend and assistant Asensio Juliá. Clad in a shabby, ill-fitting coat, the fable-teller looks down upon the world with no illusions, his bold gaze centred on something that might, given the studio setting, be a work by his master. The trace of disdain suggests his connoisseurship and critical eye – and his willingness to voice his opinion freely. As in Goya's self-portrait in his studio, it is light that plays the leading role here. Whether a dazzling *fluidum* or a diffusely Rembrandtesque chiaroscuro, it is celebrated as the *conditio sine qua non* of painting.

The predominantly brown tones of both these studio paintings express the material creation of the painting out of oil and dust or pigment. It is a process that sometimes involves hard work by the light of a candle affixed to the hat or, like Asensio Juliá, standing among scaffolding in the chill air of a church to be painted. In his self portraits, Goya never shows himself as an artist prince – just as he also portrays art connoisseurs with a certain understatement. For instance, Sebastián Martínez is seated on a humble straw chair with a relaxed dignity that merely heightens the sophistication of his singularly cultivated appearance. It is no coincidence that he is holding a print – after all, Goya had the opportunity of studying his friend's vast art collection while he was ill and staying at his house in Cadiz, where the etchings of Piranesi proved an important source of inspiration.

Goya painted more than two hundred portraits – many out of duty, some for pleasure. Portraiture brought him wealth, respect and fame in his own lifetime. After some initial experimentation, it became the vehicle for his self-assured artistic expression. The works themselves benefited from this development. The classical format, the reduction of space and costume detail in favour of increased concentration on the sitter and the casual pose are all factors that marked the end of Rococo role play and gave the sitters a strongly personal presence. Goya's portraits are never freighted with allegory and attributes, let alone with artistic sleight of hand – they are pared down to a distinctive gaze, an individually recognisable face and an appropriately incisive handling of colour. Even the increasingly free and virtuoso brushwork that some of his contemporaries dismissed as shoddiness was never used as an artistic device for its own sake, but served to heighten the brilliance and liveliness of the portrait. Many of his models grew old with him – but their portraits appear to become younger and more vibrant with Goya's increasingly confident mastery of his craft. The older Goya became, the more modern his portraits were – so modern, indeed, that such 'modern' artists as Manet would later look to them for inspiration.

Portrait of Sebastián Martínez (1792)
743 paintings and several thousand prints made Goya's six-month convalescence at his friend's home a time of study and contemplation. Goya's frequently unorthodox style of painting is evident here in the fine line of the cuff, applied with a spatula.

Light and Shade

"The world is a masquerade.
Face, dress, and voice, all are false.
All wish to appear what they are not.
All deceive."

Capricho 6, after Lope de Vega

When Goya painted his *Self-Portrait in the Studio* between 1790 and 1795 he was no longer portraying a radiant young man with flowing locks bathed in the pathos-laden light of the Baroque. Now he stands before his canvas, silhouetted against the counterlight, defiant as a torero, his stocky frame brimming with concentrated energy, his gaze fixed on the model.

The next self-exploratory work – an inkwash drawing executed with a sure hand – is an even more direct confrontation with the self and the spectator, in which his piercing eyes seem almost demonic. The tilt of the head, the upward gaze and the face framed by locks lend him the air of a lion ready to pounce – an impression further compounded by the fact that this portrait complies fully with the Renaissance notion of the 'leonine' portrait of the man of substance. This leonine aspect is a sign of strength, power and natural majesty – but also of that ancient saturnine affliction of the humours, *melancholia*. For an artist, however, it is a trait that confers the mark of genius. In the miniature self-portrait of about the same time, this creative melancholia becomes a weary, flat and very worldly melancholy. The painter is no longer painting, but is merely gazing introspectively. The lines around his mouth echo the worry lines on his brow that are furrowed more deeply still by the cold light; the lion may have aged, but he has aged gracefully. Indeed, his elegant garb might even suggest a social lion, were it not for that fact that he seems so perturbed. In yet another portrait done some four years later, there is nothing leonine left, but the look of irritation has gone; a rather schoolmasterly, bespectacled Goya looks out at us with knowing curiosity. The relaxed mouth, the well-groomed grey hair and the moss-green coat all suggest that he has become calmer, wiser, warier and more aloof.

The years that followed the studio portrait were surely both the happiest and at once the most tragic in Goya's life, overshadowed as they were by his love for the Duchess of Alba. "It would have been worth your while to have come and helped

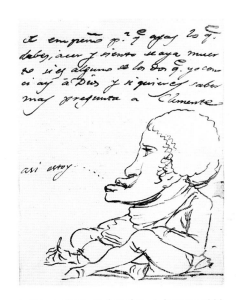

Letter caricature, London, 2 August 1800 (*c.* 1794)
"This shows how I am," was Goya's comment about this caricature of himself sketched at the end of his 'London' letter. The drawing itself is as puzzling as many of the references in Goya's letters to his childhood friend Zapater – clearly, they had some kind of shared code that can no longer be deciphered.

Portrait of the Duchess of Alba (1795)
In 1795 the duchess was thirty-three years old and had already been married for twenty years. She is shown in an outdoor setting, in keeping with the English style of portraiture, albeit without the typical verdant park-like background. Yet it is precisely the sparseness of the landscape that emphasises the capricious nature of the duchess.

Self-Portrait (c. 1795/97)
The static, iconic frontality contrasts here with the inner disquiet and bitterness of this self-portrait. The dramatic impulse and unruly hair foreshadow the Romantic era. Javier Goya chose this pen and ink drawing as the frontispiece for one of the posthumously published albums of his father's work that he compiled from existing albums and individual drawings.

Self-Portrait, 1795–97

Self-Portrait with Glasses (1797/1800)
"I have become old and wrinkled. You would recognise me only by my snub nose and sunken eyes ... I am well aware of my forty-one years, whereas you probably look just as young as you did back then at Pater Joaquin's school." Even in 1787, Goya made frequent reference to his age, just as he did ten years later in this self-portrait. Here, the process of aging is emphasised by the glasses, which indicate an admission of failing eyesight – a detail occasionally found in artists' self portraits from the eighteenth century onwards.

me paint La Alba, who barged into my studio yesterday to have her face painted, and it's now done. I definitely prefer this to painting on the canvas ..." he wrote to Zapater, dating the informative and chatty letter somewhat quirkily, "London, 2nd August 1800" and adding a caricature of himself. The distinctly casual tone of this letter written between July 1794 and August 1795 gives some idea of the impression that the beautiful aristocrat's eccentric behaviour must have made on him – he seems to have lost all sense of time and space, as the imaginary date indicates; "...and now I also have to do her in full-length," he continues, probably alluding to the pair of portraits he made of the Duke and Duchess in 1795.

These paintings composed in the English style show an ill-matched couple. While Don José leans casually against the pianoforte in a warm-hued interior, leafing through a Haydn score, the Duchess stands beneath an open sky with both feet firmly on the ground. Whereas the arrogance of the Duke is reflected in the way he turns away from the world to immerse himself in music, that of the Duchess is shown in her undisguisedly haughty and commanding demeanour, her direct yet aloof gaze and her imperious gesture, which is unlikely to be directed at the obedient little lapdog at her feet that echoes the stance and colours of its mistress like a court buffoon making jest of her.

The hauteur of the Duchess is both real and feigned, and her gaze, for all its candour, has a touch of vulnerability and melancholy, even gentleness, that is underlined by the gauzy white of her dress but countered by the brashness of her crimson sash and the shock of unruly black hair. The Duchess triggers mixed feelings – hardly an unusual basis for arousing the kind of all-consuming passion that Goya felt for her. Whether his feelings were requited is not known. There is no mention of Goya's feelings or of how things developed between them, if at all,

Portrait of the Duke of Alba
(1795)
The duke is portayed in a setting of luxury and refinement
that reflects his gentlemanly
and cultivated personality
and his preference for a quiet
life, in contrast to his wife.
His love of music and the
melancholy of his expression
suggest that the hunting garb
is little more than a device to
underline the English style of
the portrait.

in any of his letters. The Duchess does not appear in his work again until 1796/97, by which time she is a widow.

The *Sanlúcar Album* speaks volumes. The drawings tell of a life of luxury, ease and pleasure at the Andalusian country estate of the Alba family – a summer of liberty, equality and infatuation, charged with eroticism and yet, for all the raciness this may imply, somehow innocently serene. This idyll of contentment seems to have overcome all boundaries of time and place, and the drawings themselves are sketched with a freedom indicative of just how liberated Goya must have felt. They show the Duchess of Alba and her maidservants in everyday situations: from her histrionic tantrums to her maternal tenderness towards her adopted child.

This is our first encounter with Goya as draughtsman, and even though the finely nuanced inkwash shows him to be a painter through and through, never was the line so independent of the form. He retains the same vibrant brush stroke in his painting, deploying these new expressive qualities in yet another portrait of the Duchess. However great the deliberate similarity may be between the painting of 1797 and that of 1795, they are nevertheless worlds apart. With sharply drawn, deeply coloured lines, broad translucent swathes and scattered highlights in the manner of Velázquez, he presents the Duchess in the garb of a *maja*, bringing out

Duchess of Alba (1796/97)
The two drawings on the front and back of the same sheet show the front and back of the model. This whimsical and rather bold idea is a kind of precursor to the *Naked Maja* and *Clothed Maja*. Whether or not Goya was also indulging here in a parody of classical statues such as the *Aphrodite Kallipygos* remains a moot point.

the very essence of the costume itself and, with that, the nature of the wearer. Her temperament and subdued passion, shrewishness and pride, drama and melancholy have little in common with the doll-like figurine of the first portrait. It is the 'Black Duchess' that is the real Alba, and this is the real *maja* who needs no silly little lapdog at her feet when she has others at her beck and call. The artist, for instance. In that imperious manner that we have already seen her display, she points to the words *Sólo Goya* [only Goya] traced in the sand. The *maja* is by nature fickle and fleeting, her favours as lasting as the writing in the sand. An etching of 1797/98 tells us that Goya was to find this out for himself. The fantastical *Dream of Lies and Inconstancy* is bitter reality; the Duchess of Alba has two faces, and only one of them is turned towards the man who is completely besotted with her. Flighty as a butterfly, she finds helpers with forked tongues to procure other lovers for her. This act of betrayal takes place against the backdrop of a wasteland that is the dark landscape of the soul, and the dreams of the man who loves her appear as a faraway castle, a shimmering mirage, built on sand.

Goya found a way out of this emotional debacle by immersing himself completely in his work. A major commission to decorate the Church of San Antonio de la Florida in Madrid could hardly have come at a better time. The new-found boldness of his brushwork was well suited to a project such as this, given that a cupola fresco is intended to be seen from a considerable distance. The finished cupola decoration is very close to the preliminary design, both show a teeming mass of brightly coloured, boldly worked figures in a composition that is a far remove from the transcendental heavenly hosts of the Baroque. The all too human audience is as prosaic as the illusionistically painted metal balustrade and only a few of these individuals actually seems to be paying any attention to the quietly and insistently preaching miracle-worker St Anthony as he stands there before the barren, bluish-grey mountains.

Yet not even this poignant legend could give Goya any respite from the emotional turmoil he was experiencing in the here and now. His pain had made the world a colder place, and beneath the bright vitality of the surface was a dark

Portrait of the Duchess of Alba (1797)
In spite of the determined finger-pointing gesture, the words *Sólo Goya* (Only Goya) in the sand are not intended for the viewer's eyes. The intimacy of this portrait is also suggested by the name Goya on her ring and by the fact that this life-size portrait remained in the artist's personal possession until at least 1812.

The Dream of Lies and Inconstancy
(1797/98)
Seldom did Goya use so many metaphors and symbols. The two-faced woman is based on the personification of falsehood illustrated in Cesare Ripa's *Iconologia* (or Book of Moral Emblems). The etching was originally planned for inclusion in the *Caprichos*, but in the end Goya kept it for himself – presumably because of its all too obvious reference to the Duchess of Alba.

abyss that the light of reason could not penetrate. In his work, mortals appear as ridiculous and tragic figures who wear masks, brawling and fighting out of vanity, stupidity and greed, each eager for some small advantage, each wracked by all manner of imagined, acquired and deep-rooted fears. This is life in Madrid where, as in any other city, people break up and make up, lie and cheat, love and suffer. The world we live in – the world in which we feel at home by day and even by night, when the demons of the underworld come out in our dreams – seems to be in the grip of the seven deadly sins and the never-ending battle of the sexes.

The caustic *Madrid Album* follows hard on the heels of the idyllic *Sanlúcar Album*. For the first time, handwritten texts appear beneath each scene – a device that is later to become the hallmark of the *Caprichos*, that great cycle of acquatint etchings on which Goya is already working by now. It is only a small step from a collection of bound drawings to a sequence of prints. Producing tapestry cartoons had accustomed Goya to the notion of the series. A basic idea can be explored and conveyed with greater variety and richness in a sequence than in a single picture. It can be read and reflected on like literature – especially when it takes the form of prints that can be leafed through. And, like a book, a suite of prints can reach a far broader audience than one unique painting. Goya had other things in mind than churning out conventional, brightly-coloured images, and so the black-and-white print provided the perfect vehicle for his 'negative universe'. A preliminary drawing originally intended for the title page sets the tone for the series: the artist, asleep at his desk, menaced by beasts. In its contrast of light and shade, this print achieves a greater intensity of expression than any painting, while the Witch Paintings of the same time appear oddly chimeric. The transposition to the medium of etching lends a literally caustic and incisive aspect to his take on the perversity of the world. It was a technique that Goya had not practised since the court commissioned him to create a number of etchings after Velázquez. Once an idea had taken hold, one thing led to another, and Goya now began combining these motifs with the recently developed technique of aquatint which was the ideal carrier for conveying this twilight world between wicked reality and even more wicked dream, with his own wide-eyed face staring out among them. For the first forty-two of his eighty *Caprichos* Goya designed a new title page – a self-portrait that has shaped our image of him like no other. He appears in profile, his piercing gaze looking down upon the world, stoney-faced and slightly disdainful. Both in his physical appearance and his attire, he has the air of a *flaneur* watching the world pass by. He remains reservedly aloof, though not untouched by what he sees, for there is sadness and controlled anger in his expression.

For all his grumpy disinterest, he is nevertheless part of the world and its vanities, as his prints, including the self-portrait of *Capricho 1*, indicate. It is a world of ugly moods, dark vices and the dissolute excesses of a society full of self-satisfied perpetrators and their victims – victims who themselves become perpetrators at the first opportunity. Worldly bureaucrats wield their authority mercilessly, as do the Inquisition and furious mothers. The priest, the pampered aristocrat and the whore take what they can get – though the latter, at least, has learned the tricks of her trade well from the old procuress. It is a bold sequence of scenes, its mordant satire barely tempered by reworking the even more audacious preliminary studies and their deliberately ambiguous captions. *Están calientes* (They are hot) – these spiritually bankrupt monks who indulge in gluttony and all the pleasures of the flesh. *Bien tirada està* (It is nicely stretched) – the stocking as the seductive fetish of a love that can be bought, and *Que viene el Coco* (Here comes the Bogeyman) – dear children, you'd better go to bed or he will get you.

Old Beggar-Woman and Maja
The beggar-woman is very probably a Celestina, or procuress, giving the young woman some sound advice before she encounters the men sitting in the background.

Self-Portrait Capricho 1
Capricho 1 shows the artist stylising his appearance in a specific direction. What contemporary commentators described as *satirico, maligno* and *de mal humor* can be traced back to Charles Le Brun, whose influential treatise *Méthode pour apprendre a dessiner les passions*, posthumously published in 1698, presents expressions of emotion, including very similar traits for the portrayal of *Le Mespris* (Disdain).

The Sleep of Reason Produces Monsters
Capricho 43
There are several different interpretations of this drawing. One thing they all agree on is that when we dream we are visited by subconscious fears and wishes.

Están calientes
They are hot, *Capricho 13*
Here, Goya addresses the
shameless insatiability of
the clergy.

13.

Estan calientes.

The enigmatic and puzzling *Caprichos* provided no shortage of food for speculative thought at the time, as documented by a large number of contemporary reports, ranging from perspicacious to obscure and even indiscreet. The *Caprichos* proved a resounding success, albeit more as a talking-point and source of amusement than in actual sales. Announced at length in the Madrid *Diario* of 6 February 1799, the last Ash Wednesday of the century, the sequence of prints attracted buyers to the aptly named Calle del Desengaño (Street of Disappointment), where Goya lived and where his cynical outpourings could be purchased from a perfume and liquor store – appropriately enough, given that this, too, is strong stuff in its own way – for the princely sum of 320 *reales,* equivalent to an ounce of gold.

The few who could afford such an expense were wealthy, educated connoisseurs well able to appreciate the darker side of this work, the second part of which occasionally descends into real pandemonium: the sleep of reason. In a 'second' title page, the famous *Capricho 43*, the author portrays himself, in contrast to the alert observer of *Capricho 1*, asleep and dreaming, in the sleep that brings forth monsters. Goya parades them before us, these creatures of the underworld, this light-shy, diabolical pack of owls, bats and cats that are held at bay only by the tireless alertness of the lynx that embodies Reason.

"I'm not afraid of witches, hobgoblins, apparitions, boastful giants, knaves or varlets, et cetera, nor indeed of any kind of beings except human beings…," writes Goya in an undated letter, and indeed, it is not the clawed spectre that puts fear in our hearts, but the human individual who does its bidding, flirting with it and accommodating it. *Se repulen* (Sprucing themselves up) – the corrupt officials with their vulture-like faces, before they set out to hunt their prey under the bat-like wings of their superiors. Even a skeletally scrawny old woman is sprucing herself up, blinded by vanity in spite of the light and mirror – *Hasta la muerte* (Until Death). There is vanity, too, in the vapid screeching of the parrot, whose bedazzled audience sits at its feet, seeing only the opulence of its golden beak – *Qué pico de oro!* Blind and power-hungry, humankind becomes the plaything of

Que viene el Coco,
Here comes the Bogeyman, *Capricho 3*
Goya explores the theme of children's fear of night and darkness.

Qué viene el Coco.

Bien tirada está
It is well stretched,
Capricho 17
Stockings, scrutinised here
by the procuress, were
seen by Goya as an instru-
ment of seduction and
fetish of the love that can
be bought.

Bien tirada está.

unpredictable giants; flying witches keep company with fickle beauties and carry
them off as worthy aspirants to their arts. But these flights of fancy are short-lived
– unless one is devoted to the dark powers and joins their ranks, like the young
novice astride the phallic broomstick of the old crone who is described as her
Linda maestra! (Pretty Teacher!). There are witches everywhere. The wind is their
accomplice; it carries them willingly away or mockingly lifts the skirts of their
mortal sisters. There are witches behind the masks of innocence – like the young
woman languishing in a dungeon. Who might possibly have murdered her husband? The boundary between the world and the inferno is blurred in the *Caprichos*, and just as the majas become demonic furies and the high-ranking officials
become freakish monsters, the torments of hell that appear in the end are very
earthly sorrows, like the couple bound together, with inhumane law in the form of
a triumphant owl hovering above their desperate and futile cry for help.

Such satires are by no means new. Ever since Sebastian Brant's *Ship of Fools*,
literature has been full of descriptions of a world ruled by folly. Some of the

Hasta la muerte

Se repulen

Linda maestra!
Pretty Teacher!
Capricho 68
Among the obscene allusions
in this nocturnal image is the
owl – in Spanish: *búho*, slang
for a streetwalker. In its broad-
est sense, this *Capricho* is also
a satire on bad upbringing – a
contemporary commentary
points to the corrupting influ-
ences that many maidservants
have on the young daughters
in their households.

Caprichos adapt themes from the Spanish literature of the Baroque, and many of the captions are references to, or puns on, some of the sayings and proverbs that were popular in Spain as an expression of ancient wisdom and a substitute for education. The title of *Capricho 2* is a quotation from a satire by the Enlightenment thinker Jovellanos, recently dismissed from his ministerial post, and as such pays congenial homage to him. Goya was also familiar with the work of Hieronymus Bosch in the royal collections, including his table depicting *The Seven Deadly Sins*. Goya's work is the culmination of a development whose trajectory can be traced from the Middle Ages to the Enlightenment. But in the *Caprichos* the moralist looking down upon the ills of the world becomes a fearless traveller in the realms of the subconscious. It is his ability to convey these phantasmagoria that is the mark of Goya's genius. Witches, owls and hybrid creatures teem and tumble in misty twilight landscapes or settings distorted by perplexing lights and shadows. The settings themselves, if they can be described as such, are so surreal that there is no longer any need for a motley repertoire of weird and wonderful characters: the human figure itself is demonic enough. The silent hooded figure instils a deeper sense of unease than any monstrous spectre, and the shaft of light that emanates from him is sharper than any vulture's claw. The perverse trinity of truly feral officials is more uncanny than the hybrid whore-chicken they are plucking, the gaping maws of the monks more nightmarish than the witches that fly away to the sound of screeching owls.

Goya conquered this new world step by step, through a process of gradual reduction. The first thing to go was colour – to be replaced by an infinite range of nuanced shades and hues ranging from glaring light to abysmal darkness. After that, rooms or spaces and the objects within them went – in some cases there is not so much as a window, a tree or a shrub to suggest any recognisable place. But in abandoning space, Goya also abandoned the laws of art that had prevailed since the Renaissance: three-dimensionality, perspectival depth, and the logical handling of light. What

El sí pronuncian y la mano alargan al primero que llega
They say Yes and give their Hand to the First Comer, *Capricho 2*
Here, Goya criticises the arranged marriages that were commonplace in wealthy circles. Both partners are going to the altar with the intention of cheating on the other.

El amor y la muerte.

remains is a situation stripped of time and space, carried by figures that have become ciphers.

Whereas in the *Madrid Album* the dying man leans and casts a shadow against a sunlit, perspectively foreshortened wall, in *Capricho 10* there is only a dreary heap of stone blocks. They give no support whatsoever to the dying man – if anything, they support only his distraught lover, who is standing helplessly beside him in the drawing. The sense of pathos is further heightened by the abstract darkness at the upper edge of the picture that seems to bear down inexorably and insistently to swallow up the dying man. In the great eternal blackness of Death, its cause – a petulant duel – seems all the more pointless. Moreover, the pose, the slender faces and the painfully opened mouth of this couple bound up in the triviality of life echoes that central icon of Christian mourning, the pietà, with an immediacy that may well have seemed shocking to Goya's contemporaries, especially given the irony of the banal yet pathos-laden title *El amor y la muerte* (Love and Death). In their use of language, too, these *Caprichos* are works of art. Though Goya's laconic letters and his profound deafness meant that he was not a man of many words, he was nevertheless a master of the well-turned phrase. He loved puns, metaphors and ambiguities. For instance, the *Bellos consejos* (Pretty Teachings) offered by the hard-boiled procuress in matters of seduction (*Capricho*

Woman Holding Dying Lover (1796/97) (preliminary study)

El amor y la muerte
Love and Death, *Capricho 10*
The dagger and cloak on the ground suggest that a duel has taken place here, and that the young woman was the reason for it.

Bellos consejos.

15) are also pretty vile teachings that settle like a cloud of poison on her innocent charge. For all her coyness, she is dressed up for the oldest of games – or is the coyness itself all part of the game, too? *Ya es hora* (It is Time) is the title of the last *Capricho,* in which a cobold-like cleric lies yawning on the ground. It is time for them to go to sleep after the exhausting excesses of the leisures in which they have indulged in the preceding prints. It is time for a new age without hooded figures and superstitious fears. It is time to say goodbye to the all-obscuring spectres and wish them *Buen viage* (Bon Voyage) as in *Capricho 64* – and it is time at last to follow the advice of the Roman poet Horace: *Sapere aude!* (Dare to be wise). As the teeming cycle closes, one wonders how Goya's reputation ever survived publication intact, given the amount of potential fodder it supplied for any number of Inquisition trials.

In 1803, Goya gave the remaining prints of the *Caprichos* to the king, along with the printing plates. It was a smart move, and a surprising one too, considering the references contained in the works to certain high-ranking royals, among

Ya es hora
It is Time, *Capricho 80*
The series ends with one final attack on the clergy and their lives of leisure.

Subir y bajar
To Rise and Fall, *Capricho 56*
Pride comes before a fall.

Page 92
Bellos consejos
Pretty Teachings, *Capricho 15*
Often, mothers acted as procuresses for their own daughters.

Volaverunt.

them the Duchess of Alba (*Capricho 61*), who had died in 1802, the Minister Godoy (*Capricho 56*) and, possibly, in *Capricho 55*, even the incorrigibly vain queen herself. But admitting this would have meant admitting certain likenesses, and since those concerned were also capable of tactical ploys, the balance of terror was tacitly maintained and Goya escaped with impunity – though he received no further commissions from the court.

In the end, it was not his tongue-in-cheek *Caprichos* that brought Goya up in front of the Holy Office in 1815, but his paintings of the *Naked Maja* and the *Clothed Maja*, produced between 1798 and 1805. These works appear to fit seamlessly into an age in which the higher social strata married on the assumption of marital infidelity (*Capricho 2*), when any lady of substance might be expected to have a *cortejo* – a lover befitting her rank – and when the queen's own favourite might be made a minister, who would then happily host a dinner where he was seated between another mistress and his own wife. The libertinage of the ancien régime was at its height. Yet artists like Boucher or Fragonard would have been catapulted into sheer calamity had they created works that so openly celebrated the beauty of the female body, with or without the decorous mantle of mythology.

The nude was simply not acceptable in Bourbon Spain. Felipe II had been a keen collector of Italian nudes, and had commissioned Titian to paint a series of mythological scenes, or *poesie*, which illustrated the sensual charms of the body from every angle, while Felipe IV had imported the occasional titillating work by Rubens and Reni. Velázquez had painted little in this line. In Goya's day, his legendary *Venus at her Mirror* had been in the collection of the Duchess of Alba. The more prosaic Carlos III, however, bore the burden of the Hapsburg inheritance and it was his *pintor de cámara* Mengs who managed to stop the king from burning the unchaste paintings in a pique of moral outrage. Under Carlos IV, such works were again threatened by a similar fate – only this time it was the Marques de Santa Cruz who stepped in to temper his royal highness' prudence and brought the paintings to the Academy, where they could at least serve as study material.

It was around this time that Goya painted some sopraportas for Sebastián Martínez portraying young women asleep – a bold subject, indeed, in such a climate of official prudery. The chastity of these slumbering beauties is questionable, reclining as they do so invitingly on their beds of golden straw dressed only in the flimsiest of chemises. Poses like these can be traced back to antiquity, to the Roman sarcophagus reliefs of the sleeping Ariadne, for instance, but it was above all the famous marble statue in the Vatican that had been an inspiration to such artists as Titian, and which Goya himself had undoubtedly seen when he visited Rome.

Volaverunt
They have flown, *Capricho 61*
"There are heads so full of volatile gas that they need neither a balloon nor witches in order to fly." The flying beauty and the accompanying commentary refer to the Duchess of Alba, whose fickleness Goya experienced at first hand. This is the slightly less caustic replacement for the etching *The Dream of Lies and Inconstancy*.

Sleeping Woman (*c.* 1792)
For his friend Sebastián Martínez in Cadiz,
Goya painted three sopraportas showing
sleeping beauties. The obvious innocent
eroticism of the scenes corresponds to the
sophistication of the cultured art collector.

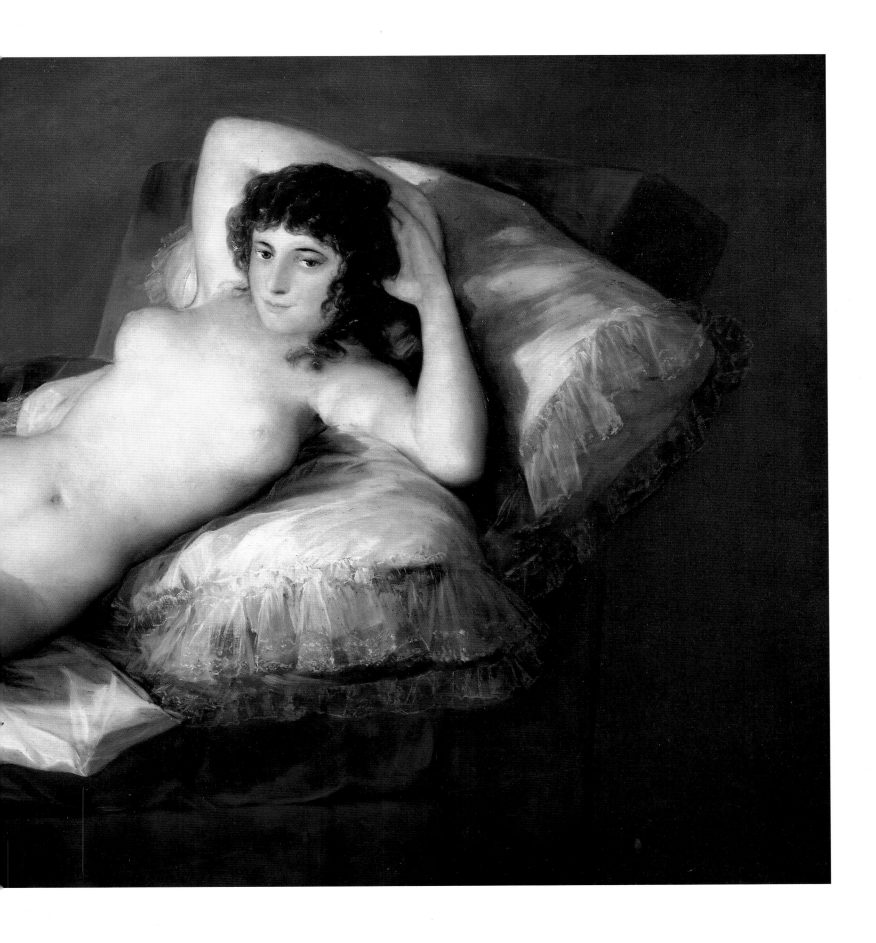

Pages 98–101
Naked Maja / Clothed Maja
(*c.* 1789–1805)

"In an inner room or cabinet there are various Venus pictures. One is a naked Venus by Goya, but without any grace of colour." The Spanish treasurer Gonzáles, the first to visit Godoy's Venus collection around 1800, is taking stock of Goya's *Naked Maja*. His derogatory tone confirms the shocking modernity of this nude. The clothed version, painted with greater brio, was added later. With it, the *Naked Maja* finally lost her status as a Venus, and on Godoy's fall from power in 1808, the inventory of his scandalous boudoir lists the paintings laconically as "naked gypsy and clothed gypsy, both reclining".

Titian had painted the casually reclining nude in the guise of Venus Awakening, but it was Goya, with his two *Majas*, who first allowed them to look the spectator straight in the eye. His *Majas* seem almost to mock the viewer, who is surely asking himself the very same questions that the Inquisition put to Goya: who was the patron, why were the paintings commissioned and what purpose did they serve? Most astonishing of all is the fact that the Holy Office seems to have had little interest in the identity of the model herself. She was certainly not, as many have suggested, the Duchess of Alba. Surely neither she nor Goya would have allowed such a nude to be added to Godoy's infamous Venus cabinet. Godoy was one of the Duchess of Alba's lovers, and had received her favours. So generously, indeed, did she favour him, that she actually gave him the *Venus* by Velázquez. To pass on an intimate nude by her ex-lover would have been quite inappropriate. It is more likely that the work was commissioned by Godoy himself; he alone could feel safe from the Inquisition. Safe enough, in fact, to feel he could install a Venus Boudoir as the centrepiece of his collection. And what could have been more irresistible than to tempt the very artist whose social ambition rivalled his own to try his skills in the sensitive territory of the nude 150 years after Velázquez – perhaps using his lover Pepa Tudo as model. Godoy as the great seducer and Goya as the artist led into temptation? Whatever the situation may have been, Goya certainly did not paint a Venus. Had ever a Venus been seen without her usual attributes, let alone a Venus that stared so impertinently at the viewer? Her gaze is utterly shameless.

This is no goddess, but a woman openly flaunting her charms. There is nothing to detract from this display of physical beauty, and the setting itself is not the usual sumptuous boudoir in Venetian red. Only a chaise longue in cool green stands at an angle in the spartan and undefined room; the naked beauty leans against a cascade of cold white pillows with controlled nonchalance. Her upper torso is displayed full-frontal, her knees coyly placed together in a way that emphasises the curve of her hips all the more. Even the slightly drawn-up thighs, while toning down the blatant frontality of the pose, actually draw attention to the pubic triangle as the focus of the image. In its simplicity and sophistication, this is a composition no less accomplished than the *Venus* by Velázquez. Goya pays homage to his great predecessor's masterpiece by presenting a clear counterpoint that provides a full-frontal view of all that Velázquez' *Venus* conceals.

The *Clothed Maja* creates a further contrast, taking the allusion to male fantasy to its very limit: same model, same pose, same sense of seeing and being seen – but this time in the form of a seductive "before" which turns the "innocent" *Naked Maja* into a woman undressed. It is a thoroughly provocative concept, irrespective of whether the two are seen together or in succession. If anything, the *Clothed Maja* is even more impertinent than the *Naked Maja*. Not only does her dress cling to the curves of her body, accentuated all the more by her sash; her little jacket, too, is provocative in its allusion to the dress of gypsy women – which also fits with the fact that she is wearing make-up. And the tip of her slipper, unlike the foot of the *Naked Maja*, is stretched invitingly towards the viewer – almost close enough to touch, just as the entire figure seems to approach and beckon the spectator. Most impertinent of all, however, is the style in which this alluring beauty is painted.

There is no sign here of the painstakingly modelled brushwork of the nude; the brushstrokes are broad, fluid and thickly layered, evoking all the sketchiness of a Fragonard without any of his ostentatious ornamentality. Goya's brushwork is as full of temperament, as vibrant and as defiant of convention as the model herself – her naked alter ego seems aloof and as cold as marble by comparison. The officers of the Inquisition knew full well why they banned *both* pictures. How Goya himself escaped punishment remains a mystery. The records of his defence are lost. But surely no artist could have been more nervous than Goya when called before the tribunal to defend his *Majas*. These two paintings were not displayed in the Prado until 1901. In the museum setting, however, it is hard to imagine the original impact of these real-life women looking down boldy at the privileged male spectator from among the idealised love goddesses in Godoy's secret cabinet.

Diego Velázquez, **Venus at her Mirror (Rokeby Venus)** (1648–51)
Goya deeply admired Velázquez and studied his *Venus at her Mirror* carefully before starting work on his *Majas*.

The Black Paintings

Yo lo vi (I saw this)
Los Desastres de la Guerra, No. 44

Goya showed what people are capable of doing to one another. Images of cruelty, violence and fear make up a large proportion of his œuvre, and it is these pictures that seem more modern than any of his others. The Inquisition, bandits and the horrors of war were everywhere in Spain, and provided plenty of material for new visual worlds. Yet it would fall short of the mark to describe Goya merely as a critical eyewitness documenting the events of his age. Instead, especially after becoming deaf, he seems to have been positively obsessed by themes of suffering, madness, marginalisation, sexuality, devouring and being devoured. Sleeping and screaming, flying and falling, captivity, mutilation, murder and loneliness are the motifs in his imaginary world of the deepest, darkest fears that lurk behind the façade of civilisation only to emerge and become reality in times of war. Goya was the first to portray the cosmic coldness of a world in which the individual stands alone, abandoned by God. In the prevailing intellectual climate of the early eighteenth century, *ratio* – reason – was regarded as the true essence of the human individual. Goya set aside the optimism of the Enlightenment and brought to light the suppressed, darker side of human nature. Yet the light he sheds on it is wan and has no warmth. It is the light of the cave, the abyss, the dungeon – real and imagined. He was for a long time the only artist to convey a sense of such universal hopelessness.

The *picador* gored by a bull, the traveller in the mountains begging bandits to spare his life, the stranded survivor of a shipwreck – all these characters inhabit the uncommissioned pictures that Goya painted in 1793/94, following his illness. While such subjects may bear an affinity with the trend inspired by Edmund Burke's 1755 treatise on the sublime, which dwells upon the insignificance of the individual in comparison with the sublimity of the forces of nature, Goya's *Yard of the Madhouse* in the same series makes a more personal statement. "I witnessed this scene myself in Zaragoza," he writes, and his depressingly mono-

Death of a Picador (1793)
Goya described the series of eleven tin-plate engravings he made during his convalesence as 'national pastimes'. Several of these cabinet pieces feature scenes from bullfights. They illustrate not only Goya's compositional skills but also his remarkable ability to portray a crowd (in this case, breathless with excitement) with just a few deft strokes.

Page 104
The Burial of the Sardine (1812/19)
In this painting, Goya unites some of his main motifs with superb compositional skill and a rich palette. The carnival scene is as superficially merry as it is deeply disturbing. While some elements recall the earlier tapestry cartoons, other elements, such as the portrayal of the ecstatic crowd, foreshadow his *pinturas negras.*

chromatic figures conjure up a nightmarish delirium of madness. Whereas the protagonists here, in spite of their direct gaze, appear to be banished into a world behind glass, the scenes portraying *Bandit Stripping a Woman* and *Bandit Murdering a Woman* bring unthinkable horrors right up close. While the coolly calculated professionality of the perpetrators and the passive submission of the erotically staged victim are redolent of the Marquis de Sade and the cave-like atmosphere recalls the picturesque robbers' dens of the eighteenth century, the handling of light lends this scene of horror a previously unknown intensity. Never was darkness so impenetrable and all-engulfing, never was light so glaring or so devoid of hope. There is no salvation, and all we can wish for is that the end will come soon to release the woman who has been humiliated and cast aside to die. Her silent scream becomes the leitmotif in *Los Desastres de la Guerra*. The shadow of evil has fallen; not everyone can see it, and only Goya can portray it. Even the exhilaration of feast-day celebrations appear as bad omens. A balloon, that symbol of human hubris and of merrymaking, suddenly appears as a sign of foreboding. In *The Colossus*, the sign in the heavens becomes an indefinable phantom – a dull and mindless force that brings darkness and devastation to the world. The tiny insect-

Bandit Stripping a Woman (*c.* 1808/12)
"Each day we take another step to hell," wrote Baudelaire, who appreciated the darker side of Goya's work. His words echo the mood of Goya's *Caprichos* which turn the spectator into a voyeur of sado-erotic violent crime.

Bandit Murdering a Woman (*c.* 1808/12)
This cabinet piece shows the outcome of the previous scene. Goya brings this harrowing scene alive with the almost abstract treatment of the rocks and with the distinction between the nervy vibrancy of the brushwork in the figure of the murderer and the finely modelled body of the woman.

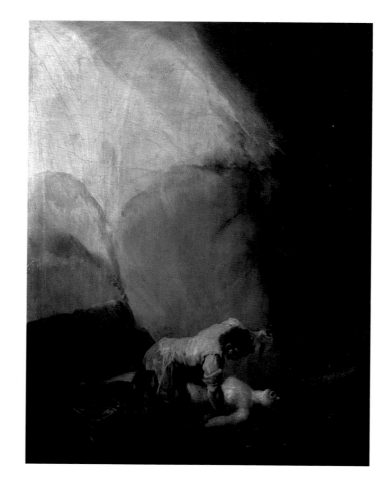

Que valor!
What Courage!, *Desastres 7*
Goya illustrates a documented incident: Augustina of Aragon took the place of the fallen men at the cannon in the defence of Zaragoza.

like creatures fleeing in panic cannot escape catastrophe, whether it comes in the form of an earthquake or a war. Reality is worse than any nightmare.

In 1808, Goya travelled to Zaragoza "to see the ruins of the city and depict the valiant deeds of its citizens," as General Palafox wrote in his invitation. Yet these deeds are just one side of the story. In the suite of etchings begun in 1810 – which the Academy later labelled *Los Desastres de la Guerra* – there is only one single scene of true heroism: the young Augustina stepping over dead bodies to take the place of the fallen men at the cannon. There are many heroes and heroines in this first guerilla war. But what kind of heroism is this that turns Spanish women into beasts and their children into eyewitnesses and orphans? And what kind of an enemy is this French army that attacks the innocent, raping and murdering, hiding behind the barrel of a gun, executing defenceless people, torturing, hanging and impaling them in cold blood? War turns everything upside down: it turns people into broken bodies, cast on the boneyard like so much garbage, making the survivors vomit.

In view of these images, *Que valor!* (What Courage!) on sheet 7 retains its cynical aftertaste. As in the *Caprichos,* image and text are indivisible, and once again the written text lends the image a certain personal touch. Reading *Para eso habéis nacido* (For this you were born) under a heap of corpses not only indicates the author's detached yet accusatory stance, but also shocks the viewer, who is directly addressed as a potential victim. Goya employs such pathos sparingly.

Page 106
The Balloon (1808/12)
This picture is regarded as a pendant to the Colossus. The two have more than just format in common. Here, too, there is a bird's eye view of a universal landscape teeming with fleeing people and animals. And here, too, the atmosphere is tensely freighted by a fateful vision in the sky. Goya probably painted both pictures for himself.

Page 107
The Colossus (1808/12)
Arriaza's poem *La profecia de los Pirineos* may well have inspired Goya to create this gloomy image. The poem, published in 1808 at the beginning of the war, is a patriotic hymn in which a giant rises from the Pyrenees to watch over Spain and banish Napoleon.

Para eso habéis nacido
For this you were born, *Desastres 12*
Surely one of the most touching of the
entire series. In this image of horror, life
seems to lose all meaning.

Estragos de la guerra
Atrocities of War, *Desastres 30*
Using an almost cinematic narrative,
the massacre of civilians is portrayed
for the first time in the history of art.

Most of the texts are laconic commentaries – their very brevity suggests the speed at which this realistic *danse macabre* whirls past, like the frames of a film which, having no cohesive storyline, constantly falls into new patterns of fragmentary horror like the crystals of a kaleidoscope. In places, the report stands still, and a variation on the same theme is accompanied by a continuous text: *No quieren* (They don't want it) says the caption to sheet 9 showing women resisting their rapists; *Tampoco* (Nor do these) says the caption to sheet 10, showing the futility of resistance, and *Ni por ésas* (Nor those) says sheet 11, showing not only the broken victim but also the perpetrator. 'I saw it, and that too' is written beneath two pictures of fleeing women, emphasising the role of the speaker.

Goya, who had learned much of this from reports, plays the eyewitness, soberly documenting events like a modern-day war reporter. Before him, Callot had distanced the horrors of the Thirty Years' War in calligraphically rhythmic scenes teeming with figures and neutral captions. Goya moves in close – encroaching upon the scene and upon the emotions of the spectator. It is as unbearable for the spectator to look at a close-up of a mutilated body impaled on a tree as it must have been for any eyewitness. Goya addresses our sense of shock in his imaging of events; one artist's proof is captioned 'The One from Chinchón'. The spectator follows Goya's path right to the very end, recognising in the figure of the impaled man a reference to the *Torso de Belvedere*. This, the epitome of the ideal physique, far more gruesomely mutilated than the marble torso, calls everything into question: humankind, our values and art itself. Like the texts, the pictures are beyond art. The means serve the end with no apparent aesthetic consideration. Place, time and space are faded out and replaced by abstract backgrounds against which the few protagonists act out their roles with their weapons – staves, sabres, bayonets, hatchets, knives, stones and ropes. The faces are unclear, distorted masks, the bodies a luridly illuminated jumble of abbreviated signs for butchery and suffering. The ciphers of violent death are endless and unchanging.

The print 'Cannot be saved any more' presents the bodies as quintessentially upright, laid low by the mechanical impact of metal gun barrels and stripped of all human dignity and individuality. The victim, as the background indicates, is only one of many. Death comes suddenly and at one fell swoop transforms a

Estragos de la guerra

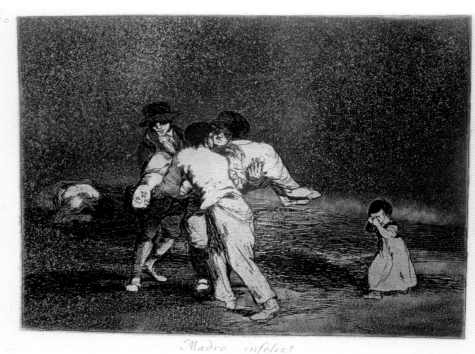

family into a chaotic heap of deformed bodies, humiliatingly exposed and more
lifeless than the inanimate objects that take on an uncanny vitality in the
surrounding tumult. The helplessly outstretched hand in the centre of this secular
Descent into Hell is echoed in the gaping mouths and fearfully staring eyes of
other victims. The head thrown back is another recurring motif – most impres-
sively perhaps on sheet 50 – and of all the children that Goya portrayed, this one,
following the emotionless figures that are carrying the body of its dead mother, is
surely the saddest. This brief scene marks the culmination of a frenzy of violence.
Now all activity has stopped. Rough horizontals and verticals bear witness to the
standstill. The abject poverty of those portrayed is expressed by a further reduction of artistic means. As in the *Caprichos*, there are references to Christian
iconography: Descent from the Cross, Pietà, Entombment. There is no irony
in the commentary on this quagmire, and in the deathly still that follows the
slaughter there are gestures of real neighbourly love. These cannot change the
cold mechanism of dying – the quiet *Beds of Death* (sheet 62) are followed by
the mass transportation of the bodies to their eternal resting place.

These scenes of death from the year 1811/12 are full of silent horror, despair,
solitude and aimlessness. They mark the end of the *Desastres* and the end of the
war. In 1812/13, Wellington's victory sealed the fate of Napoleon's army, putting
an end to the occupation. The Spanish successor to the throne, Ferdinand, having
taken every opportunity to grovel submissively to Napoleon, now began preparing

to return from his 'golden exile'. Goya felt compelled to act. Like any other liberal, he was now suspected of collaboration. What was there to prevent him leaving the country like so many of his friends?

Little was heard of Goya at this time, and following Josefa's death in 1812 he no longer had a family to worry about. There are indications that he was planning to flee – but his failure to do so suggests that it was a half-hearted attempt. Goya was no hero. Only in his art was he passionate and uncompromising. In his art, he responded with enormous sensitivity to the merest changes in the human condition. Long before the epochal change of paradigm became evident, Goya recognised that conventional values, embodied in such symbolic figures as angel, king, Venus, hero, were no longer valid. The demise of these symbols made him question the visual syntax that had been developed over the centuries for their portrayal – and this in itself may explain his resistance to classicism.

Goya did not indulge in swansong; he found dissonant new tones to express harsh new truths. A visionary and revolutionary artist of unconditional boldness, he sliced through the Gordian knot. In his private life, by contrast, he was unable to choose – he loved his home and his social position as much as his liberal ideas. He was torn between them. Once more, he toed the line, underwent a humiliating

Las camas de la muerte
The Beds of Death, *Desastres 62*
A figure in mourning watches over the victims of war.

Las camas de la muerte.

process of purification and hoped for better times: perhaps Ferdinand would accept the Constitution of Cadiz! So it was that, in early 1814, he presented his 'ardent wish' to the interim government with carefully chosen words: "To immortalise by the artist's brush the most remarkable and most heroic deeds or scenes of our valiant uprising against the tyrants of Europe" – and promptly received both money and material, having also claimed to be 'entirely without means'.

The 'most heroic deeds' he painted on the biggest canvases he had used since his portrait of the royal family were two history paintings without heroes. The events of 2 and 3 May 1808 – the popular uprising in Madrid against the French cavalry under Maréchal Murat and the subsequent execution of the rebels by a firing squad – had no names for Goya. The first scene shows a vicious struggle between soldiers on horseback and determined civilians. There is no divinely appointed leader dominating the terrain as in a Baroque battle scene. Sheer chaos rules, and the focal point is a dead Mameluke slipping quite unheroically off his horse. The battle scene is a scene of slaughter.

The second painting is, as it were, the night-side of the diptych. The situation corresponds to scenes from the *Desastres*, focused on a historical date and atmospherically condensed. The setting could hardly be more despondent: on the outskirts of the city, by night, against a gloomy hill that permits no escape, the entire scene washed by the cold light of a lantern, victims and perpetrators face one another. The poorly clad condemned man is no great, singular hero; there are many others like him, and the fear of death is written on every face. The procession is disorderly and silent – in death we are all alone. But the loneliest of all is the man kneeling in the shaft of light, his final glance directed full of dread at the well-drilled firing squad. His desperate appeal will fall on deaf ears. The soldiers in their greatcoats, like insects in their carapace, are concentrating on their bayonets. Any moment now this man's life, energised by one last burst of terror, will be extinguished, and he will lie there disembowelled like the others before him who already seem to belong to the dust of the earth. The dirty work of this anonymous bureaucratic machinery is echoed by the dirty colours of the picture and the harsh brushwork seems to express the fury of the artist as he paints – though it is a carefully considered technique diligently applied. The obvious references to the Passion of Christ bear witness to this. The kneeling man echoes the pose of Christ Crucified; the wounds on his hand mark him as a

Nada. Ello dirá
Nothing. The Event will tell, *Desastres 69*
An expression of deep pessimism and profound hopelessness.

martyr, and his fellow victims echo the poses of the mourners at the foot of the Cross. But no transfiguring ray of light descends upon him, no angel speeds its way to bring the palm frond that promises eternal triumph. The heavens remain dark, and the earthly sign of the celestial realm – the church tower – stands gloomy, stark and silent. There is no divine justice, no mercy, no redemption. What remains of the victim? *Nada.* (Nothing). This is the title of one of the last scenes (sheet 69) in the *Desastres*, whose defeatist statement was tempered by the Academy for the 1863 publication to read *Nada. Ello dirá* (Nothing. The Event will tell). But the skeleton, half-disinterred from a dusty grave against its uncanny backdrop, with the message *Nada* destroys all hope. Goya's pessimistic view of politics and the church is obvious – irrespective of whether this applied to his personal faith.

The Second of May 1808 (1814)
For all the similarity that these paintings, especially the first, may have with classical reliefs or baroque compositions, never before had war been so unequivocally portrayed as a brutal, anonymous blood-bath with no heroes.

The Third of May 1808 (1814)
The confusion and disorientation of the first scene contrasts with the coldly disciplined order of a mass execution. These paintings were not displayed in the Prado until the 1830s. *The Execution of the Defenders of Madrid* became the benchmark for all portrayals of revolution in the nineteenth century. As the image of the martyr par excellence, it was later cited by Manet in his 1867/68 *Execution of Maximilian.*

Murió la verdad
Truth has died, *Desastres 79*
A clear criticism of the regime of Ferdinand VII. Freedom is buried and only Justice mourns her lost comrade.

Fiero monstruo!
Wild monster!, *Desastres 81*
The entire cycle is summarised on this sheet. War is a wild monster that devours mankind, wreaking violence and death.

In the period that follows, we find images of profound hopelessness alongside pictures of deep devotion. Although, according to one early biographer, Goya "never completely abandoned the religion of his parents and appealed to it at every opportunity," this should be relativised, for he had clearly abandoned all ritualised piety and had no naive faith in redemption.

Ferdinand's response to his nation's sacrifices was to introduce a repressive restoration policy of such rigour that it astonished even Metternich. Almost overnight, the resignation of *Nada* (sheet 69) had become tragic reality. This gloomily prophetic etching was followed by the *Caprichos enfáticos,* which addressed the aftermath of war with the same satirically coded style of the *Caprichos.* It is a familiar game: the regal cat enthroned before devoted clerics, enigmatic as a sphynx, lending its ear to plotting owls. A fable by the satirist Casti provided Goya with the blood-sucking vampires, speaking foxes and greedy vultures that are barely concealed references to the situation under Ferdinand's rule. *Murió la verdad* (Truth has died) says the caption to sheet 79 with its elegiacally outstretched corpse surrounded by clerics solemnly celebrating the last rites. Only Justitia appears as the (powerless) companion of sacred Truth, whose light does not reach the audience – the Enlightenment has failed, and with it the freedom of the Constitution of Cadiz. *Si resucitará?* (Will she revive?) asks the next and final print, which symbolises Hope in the form of the immortal corpse radiant in the grave. In one copy of the *Desastres* belonging to Goya's friend Bermúdez, there are two additional prints at the end, which were not included in the 'standard' edition. The wild monsters, whose gluttony in devouring the victims of the human beast is an allegory of the terror of war, are contrasted with Truth resurrected appearing to a peasant in his field. With a kindly gaze, she points the old man towards a better future, which Goya perceives in the Rousseauesque return to nature. Yet this vision, like the *Desastres* as a whole, may well have been intended only for posterity. Under the rule of Ferdinand, the publication of these images would have played into the hands of the Restoration and with his *Caprichos enfáticos*, Goya would have had to face the Inquisition again.

Goya, who refers disparagingly to Ferdinand as a 'has-been', creates art of the future and for the future as a commentary on the present. But since he has to live in the here and now, he turns to the past and, perhaps in a bid to compensate for his loss of earnings with the *Desastres,* puts his energy into the more reliably money-spinning *Tauromaquia* of 1816. This suite of thirty-three etchings, initially

2c

Juanito Apiñani, *Tauromaquia,* sheet 20 (1815/16)
Many visual metaphors were used as propaganda in the war against the French. One of them was the bullfight. However, the recent bitter struggle against the French 'beast' did not possess quite the same elegance and cunning as that with which the torero in this picture taunts the bull.

Because she was a Liberal?
Album C 98
The fear of death is in the face of this young woman, bound neck and foot. Her only crime was to admit her liberal views.

planned as illustrations for Moratin the Elder's history of bullfighting, sold quite slowly in spite of the popularity of the subject matter – times, after all, were hard. Still, they probably helped to lift Goya's spirits, reminding him of his youth when, as an *aficionado,* he had occasionally swung the *capa,* while the socialite Duchesses of Osuna and Alba had vied for the favour of the torero. But those halcyon days of Spanish innocence, of hunting the wild bull in the open air, and the heyday of *majismo* when Goya had watched the *torero* Apiñani display his audacious skills, were over. The swelling albums of drawings show that the swaggering *majos* have now become war-wounded beggars, and the once-proud *majas* impoverished street traders. Though many continue to celebrate carnival with its all ludicrous Lenten rituals, they seem like madmen let loose, like painted ghosts. At one with the mask of eternal youth, they do not want to recognise the sign of the times. But time itself is all too patient, and what it has completely swept away is the old order and the combined authority of church and state. The occasional monk can still be seen taking off his habit or even working, but the plump officials are still breathing down people's necks and emptying their pockets. The Inquisition, above all, is like a many-headed hydra. And there are plenty of reasons, new and old, for its continued machinations: *Because he comes from another country; Because he speaks another language; Because he is of Jewish descent; Because he brought ill tidings; Because she was a liberal,* and so on. Not to mention such historic cases as that of Galileo Galilei – the Inquisition might succeed in bringing low even the greatest of intellects, but it could stop neither space nor time. In the meantime, the hypocritically pious Holy Office continued to interrogate those who dared to think differently, making them don the tall, pointed *coroza* dunce-cap and the *sambenito* chasuble that marked the wearer as a condemned heretic.

The Inquisition still applied its devious forms of torture for the 'well-being' of the accused, and, hard as it may be to imagine, there were still those who would willingly wear the pointed *coroza* and subject themselves to flagellation until they bled – in praise of a god borne along behind them in the guise of garish models of saints. War had taught them nothing. The world was still a madhouse, an eternal carnival, and everyone continued to play their ridiculous roles and indulge in their ludicrous imaginings. There seemed no end to the folly. As though the *Caprichos* had been too tame and surpassed by reality, Goya designed another set of follies in 1815–24: *Los Disparates.*

Goya's creative rhythm seems to repeat itself. Once again, his latest creative *furor* went hand in hand with serious illness. His *Self-portrait with Doctor Arrieta* shows the patient in the style of the Mercy Seat, kept alive only by the will and workings of the doctor to whom the painting is dedicated in an inscription of the kind normally found on votive images. As in the first title page for the

Sueños/Caprichos he appears to be hallucinating – but now the uncanny figures, instead of leaping from his mind, are silent faces waiting in the wings.

Sleep, or dream, was the original idea behind the *Caprichos*, and Goya also described the *Disparates* as dreams. They fulfil the term in a far more complex sense than the *Caprichos*. Once again, dream appears not as a flight from reality, but as a path towards deeper awareness, though this time irony and social satire are replaced by a timeless mood of quiet earnestness. Everything happens in a spectral void. The combination of unprecedentedly free etching and fine-grained aquatint creates colour values redolent of photographic negatives. In this, the prints have in common a certain quality of alienation – everything seems real and yet strangely schematic and senseless, rendering the familiar in a new and unfamiliar light. The natural scale of things no longer applies – people sit on a huge branch, but neither the origins nor the destination are clear. A rock formation seems to be made up of a tangle of bodies and men with bird-masks and butterfly-wings hover somnambulantly in the dark night, as precisely constructed as they are wildly imagined. The dreamlike character of the work is like a déjà-vu experience, its impenetrable depths impossible to plumb in spite of its seeming clarity. Soldiers flee from a giant figure like a stele, garbed like a scarecrow, lifelike in its curvature (sheet 2). A man – a cleric in the preliminary study – is cowering fearfully behind a limp yet vital figure of the Madonna that appeals to the clumsy giant and distracts him: but behind the figure which might stand for the naive optimism of the common lurk gruesome, ugly faces (sheet 4).

Because he Moved his Tongue Differently
(1815–24)
The drawing depicts a delinquent who is eavesdropping on the verdict pronounced by the Inquisition.

Disparate ridículo
Ridiculous Dream, *Disparates 3*
This is probably meant to say that all human behaviour stems from the instability of human nature.

121

Disparate de miedo
Riddle of Fear, *Disparates 2*
The uncontrollable power of fear and
panic is conveyed strikingly here – in a
confrontation with a harmless bogeyman.
Peeping out of its sleeve, and smirking
maliciously, is the face of the creature
responsible for this horrific episode.

Bobalicón
Simpleton, *Disparates 4*
Carnival processions with giant papier mâché figures, such as the one shown below, were part of traditional image worship opposed not only by philosophers of the Enlightenment but also by the Church, which feared (see the 'clerics' taking cover behind the holy puppet) losing control over its flock in its uninhibited enthusiasm.

Judith (1820/23)
The Old Testament figure of Judith was a popular heroine in Spanish theatre, embodying moral strength and courage in the struggle against foreign rule. As such, this work may well be a reference to victory over political usurpers such as Napoleon, or over 'diabolical' powers such as the Inquisition.

Gruesome, too, the horse that is about to do violence to the scared and lascivious woman. Here, in the tenth sheet, Baroque motifs such as the rearing horse or the rape of a woman have been transposed into a world whose bizarre surreality brings forth an emotional landscape in the spirit of the twentieth century – Beckmann, Picasso, Ernst and others were all to discover this 'black' Goya.

Goya was well aware of human instincts, especially their darker side: the fear of the unknown that triggers an instinct to flee, and feints that fool only oneself and take the place of courageous consciousness. Ignorance is a prison that we build for ourselves, and it takes many forms. It rears up before the uneducated in the form of sacred idols and the bogeymen of superstition. It lurks in the enigmatic metaphors of the dead and barren branch, and in the realms of pseudo-knowledge where bigots gather to nurse their wrath as they teeter at the brink of nothingness. The uneducated are kept in check by the dubious wisdom of some exotic guru, to whom they listen in semi-consciousness and lascivious stupidity. An ignorant lack of self-awareness makes soldiers fear an imagined spectre more than they fear their own bestiality – the 'beast in man' that also inhabits the horse, that ancient symbol of unfettered sexuality whose urges cannot be reined in. Classical metaphors are juxtaposed with unknown symbols which, more timeless and supra-individual than the pandemonium of the *Caprichos*, seem to well up out of the subconscious.

The twenty-two *Disparates* created over a period of nine years remained an unfinished cycle. Like the copperplates of the *Desastres*, the plates for the *Disparates* were left behind in Madrid on Goya's departure in 1824. He clearly had no thought of publishing them, even in exile. Whether they had served their purpose in helping him to work through the trauma of war or whether he regarded them as a bequest to his country remains a moot point. He also had to leave his country home with its fourteen murals. Goya had long since become his own best patron – he lived with his works, which, according to Javier, he contemplated on a daily basis. What could have been more obvious than to design an ensemble for his own house just as he had once done for the king? The oils painted directly onto the plaster correspond, in decorative terms, to the wall-sized tapestry cartoons and, like them, are loosely linked thematically. But those are the only parallels.

Saturn (1820/23)
Goya shows his monster, orginating in nothingness and chaos, aggressively devouring time and death, more strikingly by far than any conventional portrayal of Chronos/Saturn with sickle, scythe and hourglass. However, it was not Goya himself who gave this picture the title *Saturn*. In Spain, Saturn was also regarded as the diabolical master of the Witches' Sabbath and as a metaphor for absolute monarchy.

Pilgrimage of San Isidro (1820/23)
Goya had painted the feast day of San Isidro before (see no. 5). A comparison of the merry spring-time picnic scene of 1788 with this eerie procession makes the wall paintings of the *Quinta del Sordo* appear as a bitter parody of his earlier tapestry cartoons.

Underpaintings reveal pale landscapes that disappear in the course of painting beneath dark and darker scenes that come to be known as *pinturas negras*. The themes, too, are black: negative. The contrast between the lightness of the outdoor world and the gloominess of the interior must have been striking indeed. Entering the large ground-floor room, one was immediately confronted with a dream-bound, tormented *Judith,* her sword raised, without a trace of heroism, and the figure known as *Saturn,* who has nothing of a deity about him. He is a scrawny, naked giant who seems to have leapt out of the nothingness of the pictorial space, curling his fingers into a bloody, headless body. A driven cannibal, he is the grossest embodiment of Goya's repeated motif of the all-devouring. Goya delves far deeper in his exploration of the Greek myth of the Titan who devours his own children and, with that, himself, than Rubens does in his *Saturn,* with which Goya was certainly familiar. Goya's *Saturn,* for all his menacing mein,

seems powerless. Nor is there anything divine about the fear that shines in his eyes – a fear born of solitude and madness. Classical mythology and, in the case of *Judith*, Christian history, crop up again in the form of superstitious and religious practice in the *Pilgrimage of San Isidro* and the *Witches' Sabbath* on the long walls. Again, these are motifs Goya has used in the past, but now the feast-day celebrations and small-scale *Caprichos* have become expansive panoramic visions of uneasy night.

In the gloomy and undefined light, clusters of distinctly ugly people have gathered – their ugliness is the face of collective ignorance that characterises the pious and the superstitious alike. Jostling ecstatically around the goat-like silhouette of a devil, they make their way over dreary hills, their minds as deep in shadow as the scenery itself. The viewer can almost hear them chanting and humming to the sound of the idiot guitarrist, their moans and sighs filling this dread

Witches' Sabbath or The Great Goat
(1820/23)
Goya's *Black Paintings* reveal him as a
great master of dramatic expression, well
aware that the power of suggestion can
trigger far stronger feelings of horror than
realistic detail.

silence. Both scenes address the spectator directly through gaze and movement, drawing him in from the margins of this mass spectacle that reveals the perversion of the devil-worshippers and the blind piety of the pilgrims alike. Both are an illusion, and everything appears schematically.

The brushwork is gestural and raw, the paint applied thickly – Goya has created an *arte povera* of his own in more than one respect. Mouldy yellow and dirty white form wan highlights ex negativo on the black, brown and grey. The means with which he expresses his disgust at the world are deliberately rough and 'poor' – just as the figures that blindly subjugate themselves in their rituals of fear are poor in spirit. Yet the impact of these images and their potential for associative connotation, individually and collectively, are intense and rich. Visitors to the Quinta must have felt as attracted and repelled by Goya's negative cosmos as they would have been by any mediaeval Last Judgement, and may have turned away

from them to look instead at the scenes that flank the door – finding on the right a real ray of light. The young woman, identified as Leocadia, is leaning on a knoll that seems to be – as her veil suggests – a grave. Whether she is in mourning for her partner Goya, who anticipates his death here, or whether she is, in a more general sense, lamenting humanity in the grip of the powers of darkness remains unclear. At any rate, her pensive gaze also invites the viewer to contemplate the absence of light and enlightenment in a world in the throes of collective madness.

Allegory and portrait in one, she has a pendant on the left of the door – an *Old Man* whose weary gaze contrasts starkly with the frenzied excitement of the figure of *Saturn* diagonally opposite. As though already looking into another world, he is deaf to the whisperings of the demon – more deaf than his saturnine creator, Goya. In the leaden visions of the Quinta, Goya shows what a keen ear he has for the voice that comes from hell on earth. This 'monumental dialogue with the self'

Duel with Clubs (1820/23)
The peaceful landscape actually emphasises the brutality of this fight to the death
in which the simply dressed men seem to
have sprung from the very earth itself like
the seeds of evil. The message of this scene
is clear, though it could also lend itself to
a more time-specific or mythological inter-
pretation.

continues on the upper floor. Lighter than on the ground floor, the scenes here are
even darker and more cryptic. The landscapes of the four large-format paintings
are probably relics from his initial, more subdued decoration plan, but even without the figures, these barren plains, bare mountains and bizarre rock formations
would be anything but cosy. The lonely expanses of the mountain under a dawn-
ing sky turns the silhouetted *Duel with Clubs* into a drama of monumental proportion – as the mythical struggle between two rival 'brothers' or nations, or,
more specifically, as the war raging across the Pyrenees between France and Spain.
The misty landscape steeped in phosphorescent moonlight lends a ghostly quality
to the Fates hovering above – but the sharply accentuated presence brings the
feared trio menacingly and nightmarishly close. Like the figure of *Saturn*, there is
nothing idealised about the Fates. They are old, repulsively ugly and utterly
unmoved in wielding the attributes by which they determine the lot of the prison-
ers in their charge, who are indifferent to the point of stupidity. Compared with
Goya's approach to mythology, conventional portrayals are little more than costume dramas. The *Caprichos* monumentalised in the Quinta into abject grisailles
of darkness, reveal gods, idols and heroes as metaphors of brutal elementary powers that toy with humanity. In view of these images, the Enlightenment faith in
human reason appears naive, and bound to fail on any major scale. The *Black
Paintings* do not portray evil and absurdity as spawned by the devil, but on the
contrary, shows Reason as an alien intruder in a world completely ruled by irrational instincts. Together with the *Disparates* of the same period, the *pinturas*

The Fates (Atropos) (1820/23)
The three Fates hover in a wan moonlight above an eery landscape with two horizon lines. As in the case of *Saturn*, the strongly sexual component (in this case an obscenely priapic pose) has been painted over in the course of nineteenth-century restoration.

negras sum up Goya's disillusionment with the world. The Quinta had nothing in common with his comfortably furnished home in Madrid, which, according to an inventory of 1812, had some sixty seats for convivial *tertulias*. The occasional visitor to the Quinta may have felt catapulted into a laterna magica show of *Phantasmagoria* like those that were a fashionable and popular entertainment in Madrid around 1820. These horror figures flickering in the candlelight of the Teatro Principe may have inspired Goya. But Goya did not create literary figures – he created self-contained archetypes that can be understood emotionally rather than rationally or intellectually.

The *Black Paintings* are Goya's last great comment on the sleep of reason. They are the culmination of an imaginary sequence throughout his œuvre from the cabinet pictures onwards, subsuming his *Caprichos*, *Desastres* and *Disparates*. Mordant social satire and eyewitness reports of real horror have become timeless parables. Anachronistic forms of superstition have become valid archetypes of the collective subconscious, portrayed in a new, expressive visual language. The court painter of the late Rococo has become the creator of an *idioma universal* in an all-encompassing and revolutionary sense. Like the artists of the Baroque, Goya saw in everything vanity, masquerade and mortality – his ubiquitous *Todos caerán* could just as easily be a Baroque motto, were it not for the fact that Goya's universe offers no transcendental certainty of redemption. The change of paradigm in Goya's art was swift and far-sighted. Only when he had said everything there was to be said could he leave his inner exile for exile abroad – as an old man.

The Onset of Autumn

*"Although I like this place and the people, it is not
sufficient compensation for leaving one's country."*

Goya in a letter to Javier, 1824/25

For all his melancholy, Goya may also have been glad to leave the gloomy Quinta
behind him as a metaphor of an equally gloomy Spain. His *Self-Portrait* of 1824,
created twenty-five years after his self-portrait in the *Caprichos*, and with clear
affinities, shows him as a grumpy old man who nevertheless still looks at the
world with curiosity. The trait of detached disdain has become one of moody
bitterness that distracts from his fashionably casual dress. It is as though he has
taken on something of the French flair – one can more easily imagine this gentle-
man playing boules in Bordeaux than being a court painter, a mordant social
critic or obsessively wrestling with the devil. Goya did, indeed, mellow in France.

Living in freedom with Leocadia and her daughter María, born in 1814 – a
child he adored so wholeheartedly that she may be regarded to all intents and
purposes as his own – clearly did him a power of good. He drew prolifically,
experimented with unconventional techniques and, after all the demonic subjects,
turned once more to some of the genre-style motifs that he had previously
painted. As early as 1808/14 he had produced some pictures that reiterated his old
love-hate relationship with female coquetry and male machismo. Without the
satirically emphasised black-and-white of the *Caprichos* we see mysterious *majas*
looking down from their balconies, beautiful and radiant against the background
of the ubiquitous old *celestina* or in the company of dark *majos* who seem to be
on the lookout for anything that might give them an opportunity for a jealous
cloak-and-dagger drama. Youth has a cruel power; with unemotional coldness,
the proud young beauty reads a letter. She takes for granted the admiration of the
world, standing as she does in the spotlight, radiant as she is in all the simplicity
of her dress. But old age, too, has a cruel power. No fine dress in the world can
bestow radiance on its wearer – the only thing that is beautiful is the dress itself;
all that it shows is the body's decay. There are no letters either – nobody is interested any more and the only news is the news reported in the papers.

Self-Portrait (Aged 78) (1824)
"Goya has indeed arrived, deaf, old,
clumsy and weak, without a word of
French nor even a servant (and none needs
one as sorely as he does), and so happy
and eager to see the world. He stayed here
for three days; on two of them he ate with
us like a student...," wrote Goya's good
friend Moratín about the arrival of the artist
in Bordeaux in 1824.

Page 132
Majas on a Balcony (*c.* 1808/12)
Some of the genre paintings created
around 1808/12 might be seen as a
watered-down version of the *Caprichos*,
of which Baudelaire wrote in 1857, "...all
these blond Spanish girls ... getting ready
for their rendezvous or for an evening of
prostitutions – the witches' sabbath of
civilisation!" This particular motif inspired
Manet to paint his 1868 *Balcony*.

**The Young Women
(The Letter)** (*c.* 1812/14)
A comparison with *The Parasol* of 1777 (no. 26) shows Goya's stylistic and expressive development. The laundresses in the background are a recurrent and frequently varied theme in Goya's work, especially his prints. Here, they seem to foreshadow the work of Degas or Cézanne.

Time and the Old Women
(*c.* 1810/12)
In *Capricho 55* Goya mocked female vanity *Hasta la muerte*. Ten years later he created a variation on the same theme in the form of a history painting. Chronos, the God of Time, standing behind the unworthy old woman, heightens the genre motif to an allegory of the transience of life. The old woman, with her hair dressed in the style of Queen Maria Luisa, is also a reference to Spain during the Bourbon restoration.

The Forge (*c.* 1812/16)
Like *The Water-Carrier* and
The Knife-Grinder, The Forge
has long been regarded as an
incunable of realistic portrayals
of working life. A French print
showing a representative of
each of the three estates
'hammering out' the constitution of 1791 may well have
inspired Goya to create this
sketchily painted image and
would suggest an allegorical
reading with reference to the
Constitution of Cadiz drawn
up by Spanish enlightenment
thinkers in 1812.

Both these pictures are full of mocking irony and vitality. Goya's reduced palette and an unprecedented freedom in his brushwork create a brilliant kaleidoscope of colour that makes his previous works seem almost ponderous and garish by comparison. *The Forge* also seems to belong to this delightful contrasting pair of pictures. In *The Forge*, youth is conveyed by the physical strength and mental concentration of the workers; the ragged clothes they are wearing do not detract in the slightest from their potent masculinity, making these images a further fine contrast to the casually strolling woman.

Goya celebrates youth in all its beauty, at leisure and at work, and so his blacksmiths, knife-grinders, washerwomen and water-bearers from this period have in common an air of strength, energy and self-assurance. It is the imaging of a new generation – Goya is the first to monumentalise the people in the figure of the individual worker. Even in the final print of his *Desastres*, Truth appearing to the peasant suggests the vision of a better future in the return to traditional values. It is both a valediction to *majismo*, which, being as work-shy as the Spanish aristocracy, has more in common with it than a mere love of ostentation. The lifestyle that once fascinated Goya is now viewed by him in the self-citing *Disparate Alegre* somewhat euphemistically as 'merry foolishness': the dancers from the banks of the Manzanares have grown old, and their dancing little more than a merry hobbling that seems as desperate as the rancid and seedy gallants themselves. The whirling dance that implies fruitlessly revolving around oneself signifies standstill; those who do not recognise the signs of the times will be left behind – all the more so if he or she has lived life as though it were an eternal childish game. And so, the pictures of young workers that Goya produced during the war years can also be seen as an unsentimental, if transfigured, reminiscence of his own youth. In his indefatigable creativity, Goya always lived a life that was the very opposite of the subversive *majismo* he addresses here by designing a new image of youth with a new and different attitude. Just as the Enlightenment label sits uneasily with Goya, so too is the widespread notion of him as an early proponent of Socialism wide of the mark. The only unchanging factor in Goya's work is his impassioned interest in every aspect

The Water-Carrier (*c.* 1808/12)
The strong young woman stands before an empty landscape like a monument, her heroic stance in stark contrast to her menial task. In fact, like Augustina at the Cannon *(see Desastres 7)*, she is one of the young women who gave their men courage and support during the seige of Zaragoza, each making their own contribution to the cause. In this case, it is the provision of drinking water. Goya painted this patriotic work as a pendant to *The Knife-Grinder* for his own personal collection.

Learned Animal (1824/28)
This chalk drawing has been interpreted, among other things, as a mordant satire on the *letrados* – men of letters, especially scholars of law, who were often regarded, and feared, as money-grabbing pedants. This would explain the claw-like fingers, but not the slightly pained expression of introspective melancholy.

of human life. This explains how his album of drawings can encompass such diverse images as exorcism, hermits, fishermen, ice-skaters and people in a park – scenes in which there is no sign of the difficult and repressive postwar period.

Goya's Bordeaux period, more than any other, produced a kaleidoscopic mix of imagery. It is almost as though his entire life was now passing by one more time; portraits of friends can be found alongside pictures of pious monks and nuns, and drops of water poured on blackened ivory are transformed into laughing *majas* and gnarled old men, while his lithographs and paintings of bullfights are more an expression of nostalgia and homesickness than of real scenes he has recently observed. In his final albums, Goya rolls out the full repertoire of his motifs and themes one last time. Dogs with eagles' wings tumble through the air or obediently draw the carriage of a cripple, young witches and grinning old men swing on ropes in a void, women flirt, pray, work and mind their children, and men fight, brawl, drink, pray and beg. Time and again, monks and madmen appear – the monks playing guitar, eating gluttonously, repenting humbly, while the madmen seem to embody not only a sense of solitude and marginalisation, but also a strange canniness, a talent for survival, and a social critique. Whether the human individual, in a frenzy of madness, becomes an animal or whether – as in *Learned Animal* – an animal becomes human, the devil is a constant presence in Goya's visual world, albeit by now only as a weak echo of the previously shady abnormalities. In *Learned Animal* the dreaming author of *Capricho 43* and the lynx at his feet have changed places and roles – now it is the human being that has awakened as a knowing, seeing cat. And it is not the owl and the bat that he must fear, but the primitive human and the instincts that urge him to do evil.

It was probably after 1826, during Goya's last visit to a Spain under the repressive rule of the sly and sphinx-like Ferdinand, that he created his last great painting, *The Milkmaid of Bordeaux*. Once, on being asked to submit his biography for the Prado catalogue, he had provided the laconic and highly-charged comment that his only teachers were 'Rembrandt, Velázquez and Nature'. Now he seems to want to demonstrate this once again. It is a work that is far from being dryly didactic. The simple motif of a young woman against a shimmering sky has been painted with a sure but trembling hand. The bold brush strokes are juxtaposed in sketchy contouring and details that suggest movement as well as emotion in the gentle, friendly pose of the figure. The girl is alone and she seems to be listening intently to her inner voice as well as to the luminous ether – the only form of listening that Goya himself had known for many years. What she hears is clearly neither perturbing nor oppressive. It is a fluid image full of forms and figures – one of which seems schematically recognisable as her companion – but her fearless gaze banishes all menace. The devil has gone.

The Milkmaid of Bordeaux,
1825–27
In one of his last paintings, showing a
beautiful young woman, Goya has
already adopted Impressionist elements.

Biography and Works

On 30 March **1746,** Francisco Goya y Lucientes was born in the little town of Fuendetodos near Zaragoza in Aragon to the gilder José Goya and his wife Gracia Lucientes, who came from an impoverished family of the Aragonese nobility. Little is known about Goya's childhood. It is likely that he attended the Escuelas Pías in Zaragoza. At the age of 14 he joined the studio of the painter José Luzán.

In **1763,** Goya went to Madrid, where he took part in the three-yearly competition of the Real Academia de Bellas Artes de San Fernando. The jury, however, did not award the young artist's work one single point in its decision of January **1764.**
In **1766** he entered the Academy competition a second time, once again without success.

In **1770,** Goya travelled to Rome and submitted a history painting to the competition of the Parma Academy, which received at least six jury votes and a commendation. He presented himself as a student of the by now famous Spanish artist Francisco Bayeu (1734–95) from Zaragoza, a follower of the academic classicism of Raphael Mengs.

1759 Death of Ferdinand VI. Accession of Carlos III to the Spanish throne. Carlos III founds the Royal Porcelain Factory at Buen Retiro.
1761 The Bourbon Family Compact is signed. Spain enters the Seven Years War. The painter Anton Raphael Mengs is called to Madrid as First Court Painter.
1762 England declares war against Spain. Giovanni Battista Tiepolo settles in Madrid with his two sons.

1763 Spain, France and England sign the Treaty of Paris that ends the war in North America. North America is now entirely under British sovereignty.
1764 The Jesuits are expelled from France. The 'First Economic Society of the Friends of Spain' is founded.
Death of Benito Jerómio Feijóo y Montenegro, a leading figure in initiating educational reform in Spain.
1765 Death of Corrado Giaquinto and Antonio Viladomat, one of Spain's most important painters.
1766 The Esquilache Riots take place in Madrid in protest at reforms introduced by Esquilache.
1767 The Jesuits are expelled from Spain.
Initial attempts at land reform in the Sierra Morena under Pablo de Olavide.
Ramón Bayeu appointed Court Painter.
Commencement on the restructuring the Prado gardens.
1768 Carlos III introduces military conscription.
Founding of the Academia de Bellas Artes de San Carlos in Valencia and the Royal Academy in London.
1769 Birth of Napoleon Bonaparte. Spanish missionary Fray Junípero establishes the first European settlement in California.

1770 Founding of the Estudios de San Isidro in Madrid, the first Spanish educational institution with a modern teaching programme.
Death of the painters Giovanni Battista Tiepolo and François Boucher.

At the end of June **1771**, Goya returned to Zaragoza. On 21 October he received his first major commission: to decorate the ceiling of the *coreto* (little choir) of the Basilico del Pilar in Zaragoza. Completed in June **1772**, his baroque composition in the style of Tiepolo met with the approval of his patrons.

On 25 July **1773**, Goya married 26-year-old Josefa Bayeu, the sister of his teacher Francisco Bayeu, in Madrid. They settled in Madrid, where they initially lived at the home of his new brother-in-law at Calle del Reloj 7–9. During this period, he created the paintings for the Charterhouse of Aula Dei near Zaragoza. Towards the end of **1774**, on the recommendation of Bayeu, Goya was appointed an artist to the royal court.
In **1775** Goya began designing tapestries for the Real Fábrica de Tapices de Santa Bárbara in Madrid. His earliest tapestry cartoons, in the academic style of Bayeu, are hunting scenes for the dining room of the Prince of Asturia (the future King Carlos IV) and his wife María Luisa of Parma, at the Escorial. On 15 December, Goya's first child was born at the home of Bayeu.

In **1776** Goya was commissioned to design a second series of tapestry cartoons portraying popular pastimes for the dining room of the Princes of Asturia at the hunting lodge of El Pardo near Madrid. Goya and his wife moved to a new home at Carrera de San Jerónimo, 66.
In **1778** Goya published a cycle of etchings after paintings by Diego Velázquez in the royal collection. For this, he used the recently invented technique of aquatinta, which he would eventually hone to perfection. Carlos III commissioned a third series of tapestry cartoons for the rooms of the Princes of Asturia in the Pardo Palace.
In **1780**, Goya was elected to the Royal Academy of San Fernando in Madrid. The painting he submitted for acceptance was the academic *Christ on the Cross* for San Francisco el Grande in Madrid. At the end of the year, he was commissioned to decorate the cupola of the Basilico del Pilar in Zaragoza under the direction of Bayeu. Goya's composition for the cupola was heavily criticised by his brother-in-law and the church authorities because of the sketchy brushwork, which was regarded as 'unfinished' It was Goya's first public

1772 Start of publication of Antonio Ponz's 20-volume work *Viaje por España* (Travels in Spain). Mengs completes his frescoes in the Camera dei Papiri at the Vatican.

1773 Suppression of the Jesuits by Pope Clement XIV.
Architect Juan de Villanueva builds La Casita de Arriba (Upper cottage) and La Casita de Abajo (Lower cottage) at the Escorial.

1774 Death of Louis XV of France. Accession of Louis XVI.

1776 Count José Moñino de Floridablanca becomes Prime Minister of Spain.
1777 Death of Joseph I of Portugal; peace with Spain.
Rodríguez and Manuel Alvarez' Fountain of Apollo is erected on the Paseo del Prado.

1778 Carlos III decrees free trade with the colonies.
Sabatini builds the Puerta de Alcalá in Madrid.
1779 Seige of Gibraltar.
Mengs dies in Rome.
First publication of the twelfth-century epic *Cantar de mío Cid*.

1780 Banknotes issued for the first time in Spain.
Death of Maria Theresia. Her son Joseph II becomes sole regent.
Indio rebellion led by chief Tupac Amaru in Peru.

Self-Portrait (1771–75)

"Even if one is not in the least interested in art, whoever comes to Spain – whether it is to buy oranges or to look into local farming techniques, whether it is to work as a broker or as a political activist – one cannot avoid Goya: he is the best guide to the country."

Ilja Ehrenburg, 1932

The Crockery-Vendor (1779)

The Picnic (1776–88)

The Basket-Carrier, drawing from the *Italian Sketchbooks* (1770–85)

Sacrifice to Vesta (1771)

departure from prevailing classical tastes in art, albeit to no avail: Goya had to execute the frescoes according to the wishes of his patron.

In **1781,** Goya's father José died. Goya began work on the large-format painting of Saint Bernard for the church of San Francisco el Grande in Madrid, a royal commission that took him two years to complete.

In **1783** Goya created his first official portrait: the *Portrait of Count Florid-ablanca,* prime minister to Carlos III. It may well have been through Floridablanca that Goya was introduced that same year to Infante Don Luis, brother of Carlos III. At Don Luis' country house in Arenas de San Pedro (Ávila) Goya painted several portraits of the family, including the monumental family portrait of Infante Don Luis. In September he returned to Madrid. On 2 December **1784,** Francisco Javier Goya was born († 1854). He was the only child from Goya's marriage to Josefa known to have reached adulthood. The family was now living at Calle del Desengaño 1, probably since 1779.

On 18 March **1785,** Goya was appointed Deputy Director of Painting at the Royal Academy of San Fernando. For the Banco de San Carlos (now the Banco España) he painted a six-part cycle of portraits. He also created several works for the Medinaceli and the Dukes of Osuna, one of the most influential families in Spain, who remained his patrons until 1799.

On 25 July **1786,** Carlos III appointed Goya *pintor del rey* (Painter to the King). According to a letter from Goya to his close friend Zapater, this appointment was due to the influence of Bayeu. Goya celebrated his new social status by buying a gig, and from now on called himself Francisco de Goya. In the period that followed he painted a cycle showing the four seasons for the royal tapestry works and eight wall paintings in the same style for the country residence of the Dukes of Osuna. In September he created three paintings for the Monastery of Santa Ana in Valladolid.

1782 Founding of the Banco de San Carlos (later Banco de España) by the French financier François Cabarrus.
The Duke of Alba commissions Juan Pedro Arnal to build the Buenavista Palace.

1783 The Treaty of Versailles between England, France and Spain recognises the independence of the United States of America.
Birth of the South American revolutionary and statesman Simón Bolívar.
Count Aranda, Spanish ambassador to France, draws up a plan for establishing independent kingdoms in Spanish America.

1784 Birth of the Infante Fernando, later Ferdinand VII of Spain.

1786 Zaragoza connected to the imperial water system.
1787 Constitution of the United States of America drawn up.
Junta Suprema (Supreme Assembly) created in Madrid.
Founding of the Colegio de cirugía (College of Surgery) in Madrid.

The Summer (1786/87)

The Drunken Mason (1786) **The Injured Mason** (1786/87)

Two Cats Fighting (1786/87)

"He is the national painter *par excellence*, who seems to have been born to the task of capturing on canvas the last traces of old customs that are rapidly disappearing."

Théophile Gautier, 1838

The Flower Girls (1786–87)

In **1788**, Goya created three oil paint-ings for the chapel of the Dukes of Osuna in the Cathedral of Valencia. He also began work on a series of tapestry cartoons for the bedroom of the Infantas, which were interrupted by the death of Carlos III on 14 December.

In **1789**, the new King Carlos IV and his wife María Luisa appointed Goya their *pintor de cámara*. He was also commissioned to paint several por-traits of the royal family. In the same year, he also painted a family portrait of the Duke of Osuna and his chil-dren. In spite of instructions from the king, Goya, refused to continue designing tapestry cartoons, a task he considered beneath him. In **1791**, he created his last work for the Real Fábrica de Tapices.

In **1792**, Goya visited Andalusia for the first time. While he was there, he fell seriously ill and suffered progres-sive loss of hearing. Up to **1794** he created a group of cabinet pieces and several portraits of the Duchess of Alba.

Francisco Bayeu died in **1795**. Goya was appointed Director of Painting at the Real Academia de San Fernando. He received his first commission from the House of Alba: full-length portraits of the Duke and the Duchess of Alba (*Duchess of Alba in White*).

In **1796** Goya visited Andalusia again. From July he stayed at the country home of the Duchess of Alba in Sanlúcar de Barrameda. The por-trait of the Duchess of Alba in Black was
created at this time.

In **1797**, Goya returned to Madrid and began preliminary studies and etchings for his *Caprichos*. Up to 1798 he created his six paintings of witches and devils for the Osuna country
residence of La Alameda.
Goya was commissioned to fresco the church of San Antonio de la Florida, Madrid, unviled in July 1799. At the same time he completed the *Mocking of Christ* for the Cathedral of Toledo.

1788 Death of Carlos III. Accession of Carlos IV.
Francisco Bayeu becomes Director of Painting at the Academia de San Fernando .
The Royal Porcelain Factory at Buen Retiro is granted permission to market its wares commercially.
1789 French Revolution.
14 July: Storming of the Bastille. Declaration of Human Rights. Spanish parliament repeals the Salic Law introduced by Felipe V.
1790 Floridablanca resists the dis-semination of French revolutionary ideas in Spain.
The *Encyclopédie* is banned. Spanish citizens are not allowed to travel abroad.
In France: church property nation-alised.
Death of Emperor Joseph II of Austria; accession of Leopold II.

1792 Floridablanca ousted; Count Aranda becomes Prime Minister and is succeeded by Manuel Godoy the same year.
French Republic declared. Begin-ning of the Jacobine Terrror under Danton.
The Zaragoza School of Drawing becomes an Academy (Academia de San Luis).
1793 Execution of Louis XVI and Marie Antoinette; state mourning declared in Madrid. France de-clares war against Spain.
1794 Danton and Robespierre beheaded.
1795 Treaty of Basle ends hostili-ties between France and Spain. Godoy is given the title 'Principe de la Paz' (Prince of the Peace). Government by the Directory established in France.
1796 Treaty of San Ildefonso: Franco-Spanish Alliance. Napoleon's Italian campaign.

1797 Jovellanos becomes Spanish Minister of Justice.

Because She Was Susceptible, *Capricho 32*

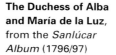
Por que fue sensible.

The Duchess of Alba and María de la Luz, from the *Sanlúcar Album* (1796/97)

First preparatory drawing for *Capricho 43*

The Devil's Incantation (1797/98)

The Puppet (1791/92)

"Goya discovered his genius the day
he dared to stop painting to please."

André Malraux, 1928

The Comedians (1793)

On 6 February **1799** the newspaper Diario de Madrid announced the publication of the *Caprichos*. In September and October he created portraits of the king in hunting garb and the queen in black mantilla. On 31 October Goya was appointed *primer pintor de cámara* (First Court Painter).

In the spring of **1800,** Goya followed the court to Aranjuez. In the months that followed he created his famous group portrait of the Family of Carlos IV.

In **1802** the Duchess of Alba died. Goya designed her tomb. In the following years up to 1808, Goya painted several portraits. In **1803,** fearing the Inquisition, he handed the printing plates over to the king.

In **1805** Goya's son Javier married Gumersinda Goicoechea, the daughter of a wealthy Madrid businessman. Goya's grandson Mariano was born the following year. As a member of the Academy, Goya swore 'loyalty and obedience' to Joseph Bonaparte in **1808**. Between two sieges of Madrid by Napoleonic troops, he travelled to Zaragoza.

1798 Godoy resigns and is succeeded by Francisco Saavedra.

1800 Urquijo dismissed; Godoy returns to power.
1801 Jovellanos in exile on Mallorca.
War of the Oranges: Carlos IV declares war on Portugal with French support.
1802 Treaty of Amiens, Napoleon's first major political achievement, brings peace between England, France, Spain and Holland.
1803 Godoy signs agreement of neutrality in Paris and uses it to enforce neutrality on Portugal.
1804 At the insistence of France, on the basis of the Treaty of Ildefonso, Spain declares war on England.

1805 Nelson defeats the Franco-Spanish fleet at Trafalgar.
1807 The Franco-Spanish Treaty of Fontainebleau gives France access to Portuguese territory. Godoy receives the title 'Principe de los Algarves'.
1808 Napoleon invades Spain. The Spanish War of Independence begins. The Riot of Aranjuez topples Godoy.
Carlos IV is forced to abdicate in favour of Fernando VII.
Napoleon makes his brother Joseph Bonaparte King of Spain.
2 May: popular uprising in Madrid (Dos de Mayo). Start of resistance against the French.
French troops defeated at the Battle of Bailén (15 July). Napoleon leads troops against Spain and occupies Madrid.

Portrait of Francisca Sabasa García (1804–08)

The Arrest of Christ (1798)

Agriculture (1797–1800)

Maja and Celestina (1808–12)

Portrait of the Marquesa de Lazán (*c.* 1804)

Micacle of St Anthony of Padua (1798)

"… a scratchy line here, a black blob there, and a white line giving contours to a person who lives and dies and whose face becomes indelibly engraved on our mind."

Théophile Gautier, 1838

Giltheads (1808–12)

In **1810,** Goya began work on the *Desastres de la Guerra*, a series of 82 etchings, most of them probably done in the years 1812–14. The prints were published posthumously by the Academy of San Fernando. In 1810, Goya was commissioned to paint an allegory of the City of Madrid in honour of Joseph Bonaparte, who awarded Goya the Royal Order of Spain the following year.
On 20 June **1812,** Goya's wife Josefa Bayeu died. An inventory of their belongings was drawn up and the estate divided between Goya and his son. Javier received the parental home and all the paintings.

In **1814,** funded by the government, Goya painted *The 2nd of May 1808* and *The 3rd of May 1808*, which adorned one of the triumphal arches when the king entered Madrid. On 2 October of the same year, Goya's young partner Leocadia Weiss gave birth to a daughter who was christened María del Rosario Weiss († 1843). Goya's paternity was never definitively established. In November Godoy's collection of paintings was inspected by the Holy Office. It included the *Naked Maya* and the *Clothed Maya*. Because of the allegedly lewd character of these works, Goya was called before the Inquisition in **1815.**
In **1816** the *Tauromaquia* was published – a cycle of 33 etchings showing the history of bullfighting.
In **1818,** Goya made the altar painting of Saints Rufina and Justa for the Cathedral of Sevilla.

1809 2nd Seige of Zaragoza; 1st Seige of Gerona.
The Duke of Wellington is put in command of British troops in Portugal.
1810 First assembly of the Cortes de Cádiz.
Miguel Hidalgo, a Catholic priest in the village of Dolores, leads the Mexican struggle for independence.
1812 Spain's first liberal constitution.
French defeated by British and Spanish troops at the Battle of Salamanca.
1813 Chilpancingo congress declares Mexico independent from Spain.

1814 Napoleon abdicates at Fontainebleau; exile in Elba.
Return of the Bourbons; Louis XVIII restored to the French throne. Jesuit Order re-established by Pius VII.
In Spain: restoration of absolute monarchy. Ferdinand VII abolishes the constitution, reinstates the Inquisition and closes theatres, universities and publishing houses.
1815 Return of Napoleon, who is finally defeated at Waterloo. Congress of Vienna: national boundaries of Europe redrawn. 'Holy Alliance' of European monarchs.
1816 Congress of San Miguel de Tucumán: Argentina declares independence.

The daring Martincho in the ring at Saragossa, *Tauromachia 18*

Sad forebodings of what is to come, *Desastres 1*

The Colossus, *c.* 1810–18

This is worse, *Desastres 37*

Procession of Flagellants on Good Friday (*c.* 1812–19)

Truth, Time and History
(1812/13)

"Goya, nightmare crammed with unfathomable things,
which roasting foetuses in a pan,
crones at a mirror served by naked girls
who straighten stockings to entice the Fiend."

Charles Baudelaire, *Les Fleurs du Mal*, 1857

The Madhouse (*c.* 1812–19)

On 27 February **1819**, Goya bought a country house on the banks of the Manzanares near Madrid – the so-called Quinta del Sordo (House of the Deaf Man), where he lived with Leocadia and little María del Rosario. In the winter, Goya fell ill. His friend and physician Arrieta looked after him. Once he had recovered, Goya expressed his gratitude in a self-portrait showing him pained and suffering in the arms of his friend. Goya began to experiment with the technique of lithography. In the period 1820–1823 he created his *Pinturas negras* (Black Paintings) to decorate the Quinta del Sordo and his cycle of *Los Disparartes* (Follies), which were not published until 1864 by the Royal Academy of San Fernando under the title *Los Proverbios* (Proverbs). On 17 September 1823, Goya gave his country house to his grandson Mariano.

From January to April **1824**, Goya went into hiding at the home of his friend Duaso y Latre for political reasons. On 2 May he asked Ferdinand VII for permission to spend six months in Plombières, France, for the good of his health. At the beginning of June, Goya left Spain and made his way to Paris, where he stayed for two months. In September he returned to Bordeaux, where he settled with Leocadia and her two children (she had a son from a previous marriage), who had followed him from Spain. In the winter months, Goya painted some 40 miniatures on ivory, which he mentions in a letter to his friend Joaquín Ferrer. In **1825**, he created the cycle of four prints known as *The Bulls of Bordeaux*.

In **1826**, Goya travelled to Madrid to ask Ferdinand VII to allow him to enter paid retirement. His petition was granted. The reason for his second visit to Madrid in the summer of **1827** is unclear.
Paralysed since 2 April, Goya died in the night of 15 to 16 April **1828** in Bordeaux.

Goya's remains were transferred from Bordeaux to Madrid in 1901 and were buried in the church of San Antonio de la Florida, Madrid, in 1919.

1820 Major Rafael del Riego y Núñez reinstates the constitution of 1812.
1821 Napoleon dies on St Helena.
1822 Antonio José de Sucre defeats the royalists at the Battle of Pichincha, ending Spanish rule in Ecuador.
Brazil declares independence: Pedro I crowned emperor.
1823 Louis XVIII sends troops to help Ferdinand VII secure his absolute monarchy. Riego executed in Madrid.

1824 Prime Minister Céan Bermúdez introduces a phase of liberal politics in Spain.
Trades unions legalised in Britain.
Death of Louis XVIII of France, accession of Charles X.
Mexico becomes a republic.
Peru: Battle of Ayacucho finally breaks Spanish influence in South America.

1825 Founding of the Republic of Bolivia with de Sucre as the country's first president.

1827 Revolt of the Malcontents in Catalonia.
1828 National heroine Mariana Pineda is executed for expressing her liberal sympathies (by embroidering a liberal banner).

Loyalty, *Disparates 17*

The Road to Hell (1819)

A way of flying, *Disparates 13*

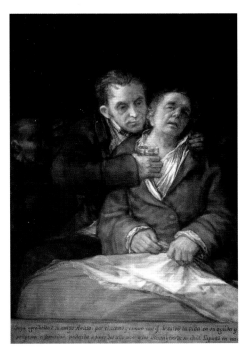

Self-Portrait with Dr. Arrieta (1820)

Christ on the Mount of Olives (1819)

"Old Spanish art died with Goya. Velázquez's
light, El Greco's devilish colours,
the traditions and customs of bullfights,
majas, manolas, the police, smugglers,
thieves, gypsies and then, to top all these,
the witches – those Spanish witches who are
that much more satanic than our own – all
came to a head and have died with Goya."

Baron Taylor, *c.* 1830

Old man on a swing, *Album H. 58* (1824–28)

Asmodea (1820–23)

List of Illustrations

Selected Bibliography

Page 151 bottom
The Madhouse, *c.* 1812–19, oil on wood, 45 x 72 cm, Real Academia de bellas Artes de San Fernando, Madrid

Page 152 top
Loyalty, *Disparates 17*, 1820–24, etching and aquatint, 24.5 x 35 cm

Page 152 centre
The Road to Hell, 1819, China ink, 18.8 x 26.7 cm, Biblioteca Nacional, Madrid

Page 152 bottom
Modo de volar / A way of flying, *Disparates 13*, 1820–24, etching and aquatint, 24.5 x 35 cm

Page 153 top left
Self-Portrait with Dr. Arrieta, 1820, oil on canvas, 115 x 80 cm, The Minneapolis Institute of Art, Minneapolis

Page 153 top right
Christ on the Mount of Olives, 1819, oil on wood, 47 x 35 cm, Escuelas Pías, Madrid

Page 153 bottom left
Asmodea, 1820–23, oil on plaster mounted on canvas,123 x 266 cm, Museo del Prado, Madrid

Page 153 bottom right
Old man on a swing, *Album H. 58*, 1824–28, black chalk, 19 x 15.1 cm, Hispanic Society, New York

Bareau, J.W. (ed.), *Goya's Prints: The Tomás Harris Collection in the British Museum*, London 1981

Blackburn, J., *Old Man Goya*, London 2002

Blas Benito, J., *El libro de los desastres de la guerra*, Madrid 2000

Buendía, R., *Goya joven (1746–1776) y su entorno*, exhib. cat., Zaragoza 1986

Brown, J. and R.G. Mann, *Spanish Paintings of the Fifteenth through Nineteenth Centuries*, exhib. cat., Washington, D.C. 1990

Camón Aznar, J., *Franscisco de Goya*, 4 vols., Zaragoza 1984

Céan Bermúdez, *L' Art européen á la cour d' Espagne au XVIII siècle*, exhib. cat., Bordeaux / Paris / Madrid 1979–80

Céan Bermúdez, *De Greco à Picasso*, exhib. cat., Paris 1987

de Angelis, R., *L'opera pittorica completa di Goya*, Milan 1974

Gállego, J., *Goya en las colecciones madrileñas*, exhib. cat., Madrid 1983

Gallego, J., Fuentes, A.E. Pérez Sánchez, *Goya: Europalia 85 España*, exhib. cat., Brussels 1985

Gallego, J. et al., *Goya, 1746–1828*, exhib. cat., Venice 1989

Gassier, P. (ed.), *Francisco Goya: Drawings: The Complete Albums*, New York 1973

Gassier, P. (ed.), *Goya dans les collections suisses*, exhib. cat., Martigny 1982

Glendinning, N. (ed.), *Goya, la década de los Caprichos, retratos 1792–1804*, exhib. cat., Madrid 1992

Hughes, R., *Goya*, New York 2003

Lafuente Ferrari, E., *Goya: Dibujos*, Madrid 1980

Lafuente Ferrari, E., *Goya en las colecciones madrileñas*, exhib. cat., Madrid 1983

Lafuente Ferrari, E., *Los Caprichos de Goya*, Barcelona 1978

López-Rey, J., 'Chronique des arts: Espagne', in *Gazette des Beaux-Arts* 115 (1980): 14

Muller, P.E. (ed.), *Goya's 'Black'Paintings: Truth and Reason in Light and Liberty*, New York 1984

Roetting, P. et al., *Von Dürer bis Goya*, exhib. cat., Hamburg 2001

Rose-de Viejo, I., *Goya / Rembrandt, la mémoire de l'oeil*, exhib. cat., Geneva 1993

Symmons, S., *Goya: A Life in Letters*, London 2004

Symmons, S., *Goya in Pursuit of Patronage*, London 1988

Tomlinson, J.A., *Francisco Goya:The Tapestry Cartoons and Early Career at the Court of Madrid*, Cambridge 1989

Tomlinson, J.A., *Francisco Goya y Lucientes*, London 1994

Tomlinson, J. A. (ed.), *Goya: Images of Women*, exhib. cat., Madrid / Washington 2001

Tomlinson, J.A., *Goya in the Twilight of the Enlightenment*, New Haven / London 1992

Walker, J., *National Gallery of Art, Washington*, rev. ed., New York 1984

Wilson–Bareau, J. (ed.), *Goya, la década de los Caprichos, dibujos y aguafuertes*, exhib. cat., Madrid 1992

Wilson-Bareau, J. and M. B. Mena Marqués (eds.), *Goya, Truth and Fantasy: The Small Paintings*, exhib. cat., Madrid / London / Chicago 1994

Wolf, R. (ed.), *Goya and the Satirical Print in England and on the Continent, 1730–1850*, exhib. cat., Boston, MA, New York 1991

Wolf, R., *Goya, toros y toreros*, exhib. cat., Arles 1990

Index

Front cover and slipcase: *Self-Portrait in the Studio*
(detail; 1790–95), see page 36
Back cover: *The Puppet* (detail; 1791/92), see page 147

The Library of Congress Cataloguing-in-Publication data is available; British Library Cataloguing-in-Publication Data: a catalogue record for this book is available from the British Library; Deutsche Bibliothek holds a record of this publication in the Deutsche Nationalbibliografie; detailed bibliographical data can be found under: http://dnb.ddb.de

© Prestel Verlag, Munich · Berlin · London· New York, 2004

Prestel books are available worldwide. Please contact your nearest bookseller or one of the following Prestel offices for information concerning your local distributor:

Prestel Verlag
Königinstrasse 9, 80539 Munich
Tel. +49 (89) 38 17 09-0; Fax +49 (89) 38 17 09-35

Prestel Publishing Ltd.
4 Bloomsbury Place, London WC1A 2QA
Tel. +44 (020) 7323-5004; Fax +44 (020) 7636-8004

Prestel Publishing
900 Broadway, Suite 603, New York, NY 10003
Tel. +1 (212) 995-2720; Fax +1 (212) 995-2733

www.prestel.com

Translated from the German by Ishbel Flett, Edinburgh
Edited by Christopher Wynne
Editorial assistance: Danko Szabó, Munich
Design and layout: Horst Moser, independent Medien-Design, Munich
Production: Ulrike Schmidt
Origination: ReproLine Mediateam, Munich
Printing and binding: Print Consult, Munich

Printed on acid-free paper

ISBN 3-7913-3071-3

Photographic Credits

The illustrations in this publication have been kindly provided by the museums, institutions and archives mentioned in the captions, or taken from the Publisher's archives, with the exception of the following:

AKG, Berlin: pp. 5, 31, 57, 153 top left
Artothek: pp. 49, 132 / Joachim Blauel – Artothek: pp. 3, 143 top / Peter Willi – Artothek: pp. 126/127, 128/129
The Bridgeman Art Library: pp. 9, 13, 24, 27, 32, 48, 71, 78 right, 79, 85, 87, 89, 92, 94, 109, 110, 112, 113, 119, 122, 123, 144/145 top left, 147 bottom left
Courtesy Hispanic Society New York: pp. 7, 81, 153 right
Archivo Oronoz, Madrid: pp. 21, 23, 37, 38 bottom, 56, 62, 96/97, 108, 143 bottom right, 147 top left
© Scala, Florence 2004: front cover, pp. 11, 16, 27, 28, 34, 36, 39, 42/43, 47, 50, 52, 60, 61, 68, 72/73, 76, 54/55, 58/59, 104, 107, 115, 117, 124, 125, 130, 131, 139, 140, 148 centre, 152 bottom